Young People's Science Encyclopedia

Em

Embryophyta
Emerald
Emphysema
Emulsion

En

Endangered species
Endive
Endocrine glands
Endoderm
Endoscope
Endothermic
Energy
Energy crisis
Engine
Engineering
Entomology
Environment
Enzymes

Ep

Epidemic
Epilepsy
Epiphyte
Epithelial tissue
Epoch

Eq

Equation
Equator
Equilibrium
Equinox

Er

Era
Erbium
Erg
Erosion

Es

Escarpment
Esker
Essential oils
Ester
Estivation
Estrogen
Estrous cycle
Estuary

Et

Ether
Ethology
Ethyl
Ethylene

Eu

Eucalyptus
Euglena
Euonymus
Europe
Europium
Eutrophication

Ev

Evaporation
Evergreen
Evolution
Evolution of man

Ex

Exclusion
  principle
Excretory system
Exoskeleton
Exothermic
Expansion
Experiment
Explosives
Extinction
Extremities

Ey

Eye
Eye, binocular
Eye, compound
Eye, simple

Fa

Fabré, Jean
Fahrenheit
Faint
Falcon
Falling bodies
Fallout
Fallow
Farad
Faraday, Michael
Farsightedness
Fat
Fat, adipose
  tissue
Fatigue
Fatty acids
Faulting
Fauna

Fe

Feather
Feldspar
Fennel
Fermentation
Fermi, Enrico
Fermium
Ferns
Fertilization
Fertilizer
Fetus
Fever

Fi

Fiber
Fibiger, Johannes

Fibrous tissue
Field, Cyrus
Fig
Filaria
Film
Filter
Fin
Finch
Fiord
Fir
Fire
Fire extinguisher
First aid
Fischer, Emil
Fischer, Hans
Fish
Fission
Fittonia

Fl

Flagella
Flamingo
Flatfish
Flea
Fleming, Sir
  Alexander
Fleming, Sir
  Sanford
Flesh
Flicker
Flight,
  principles of
Flood
Flory, Paul
Flotation
Flounder
Flour
Flower
Fluid
Fluorine
Fluorite
Fluorocarbons
Fluoroscope
Fly
Flycatcher

YOUNG PEOPLE'S
SCIENCE ENCYCLOPEDIA

Edited by the Staff of
NATIONAL COLLEGE OF EDUCATION, Evanston, Illinois

ASSOCIATE EDITORS

HELEN J. CHALLAND, B.E., M.A., Ph.D.
  Chairman, Division of Natural Sciences
National College of Education,
Evanston, Illinois

DONALD A. BOYER, B.S., M.S., Ph.D.
  Science Education Consultant, Winnetka
Public Schools, Winnetka, Illinois
Science, National College of Education

EDITORIAL CONSULTANTS
ON THE STAFF OF NATIONAL COLLEGE OF EDUCATION

Elizabeth R. Brandt, B.A., M.Ed.
Eugene B. Cantelupe, B.A., M.F.A., Ph.D.
John H. Daugherty, B.S., M.A.
Irwin K. Feinstein, B.S., M.A., Ph.D.
Mary Gallagher, A.B., M.A., Ph.D.
Beatrice S. Garber, A.B., M.S., Ph.D.
Hal S. Galbreath, B.S. Ed., M.S.
Arthur J. Hannah, B.S., M.Ed., Ed.D.

Robert R. Kidder, A.B., M.A., Ph.D.
Jean C. Kraft, B.S., M.A., Ph.D.
Elise P. Lerman, B.A., B.F.A., M.F.A.,
Mary M. Lindquist, B.A., M.A., Ph.D.
Mary-Louise Neumann, A.B., B.S.L.S.
Lavon Rasco, B.A., M.A., Ph.D.
Bruce Allen Thale, B.S.Ed., M.S.Ed.
Fred R.Wilkins, Jr., B.A., M.Ed., Ph.D.

SPECIAL SUBJECT AREA CONSULTANTS

Krafft A. Ehricke, B.A.E., H.L.D.
Benjamin M. Hair, A.B., M.D.
Charles B. Johnson, B.S., M.A., M.S.
Raymond J. Johnson, B.B.A., M.Ed.

H. Kenneth Scatliff, M.D.
Eleanor S. Segal, M.D.
Paul P. Sipiera, B.A., M.S.
Ray C. Soliday, B.A., B.S., M.A. (Deceased)

Don Dwiggins, Aviation Editor

THE STAFF

Project Director   Rudolph A. Hastedt
Project Editor   M. Frances Dyra
Senior Editor   Jim Hargrove
Editorial Assistant   Janet Zelasko

Young People's
SCIENCE
Encyclopedia

Edited by the Staff of
NATIONAL COLLEGE OF EDUCATION
Evanston, Illinois

Volume 7/Em-Fl

CHILDRENS PRESS ™
CHICAGO

Photographs

Page 2: Skylab space station (NASA)

Page 3: *Top to Bottom:*
Wheatfield (U.S.D.A. Photo)
Technician capping Abbokinase (Abbott Laboratories)
Spider (Macmillan Science Company)
View of Earth (NASA)
Space Shuttle (NASA)
Bahama coral reef (Macmillan Science Company)

Cover: Design by Sandra Gelak
Cliff Palace, Mesa Verde (James P. Rowan)
Porkfish, Shedd Aquarium (James P. Rowan)
Hepatica (James P. Rowan)

Library of Congress Catalog Card Number: 67-17925

SOME EMBRYOPHYTES

1—HORSETAIL

2—BLACK-EYED SUSAN

3—LIVERWORT

4—DEERHORN CACTUS

5—SILVER MAPLE

6—CLUB MOSS

7—FERN

8—FIR TREE

9—MOSS

Embryophyta (em-bree-AH-fuh-tuh) There are over 350,000 plants classified in the world today. They are divided into two subkingdoms. The first, THALLOPHYTA, has ten divisions of algae, fungi, and bacteria. All the rest, over 250,000 higher plants, are classified as embryophytes. They have been grouped in five to eight major divisions, from the mosses to the flowering plants.

Embryophytes range in size from very tiny plants to towering trees. Almost all have chlorophyll. A very few of them are parasites or saprophytes. Every color in the spectrum is represented in this group. They possess various pigments—the chlorophylls, carotene, and xanthophyll. They are found in water, in air, and on land from pole to pole. Most of them are terrestrial, but some of them are aquatic.

The primary cell wall is composed mainly of cellulose and pectin. All except the bryophytes have special conducting tubes. These are called xylem and phloem cells. All em-

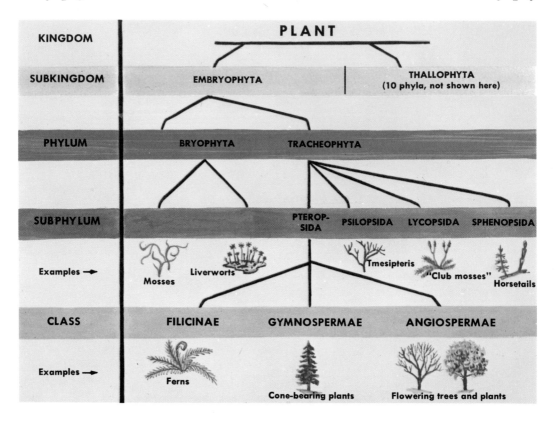

bryophytes store starch in various plant parts. Locomotion is confined to the sperms possessing moving flagella. The lower plants in this subkingdom have no true roots, stems, leaves, flowers, or fruits. Almost all have stomates and guard cells, those parts specialized for the intake of gases and the ultimate loss of water through transpiration.

An embryophyte, as the name implies, has an embryo. This is a mass of cells formed from a fertilized egg. It is the young sporophyte before it matures. Plants on land require protection for the sex cells or gametes. The embryophytes have multicellular and more elaborate sex organs than lower plants. They always produce asexual spores whereas the thallophyte's spores are asexual and sexual. ALTERNATION OF GENERATIONS is well developed. As you move from the simpler plants to the more complex, the generation which is most prominent changes. In mosses the gametophyte is larger with sporophyte parasitic on it. In the highest plants the sporophyte is large and independent with the gametophyte being the small dependent one in the cycle.

One group of embryophytes, the Bryo-

phyta, includes horned liverworts, liverworts, and the mosses. They are among the first land plants. The differentiation in structure is about the same as most of the complex algae. They have simple water-conducting cells but not true vascular tissue. They lack a cuticle for protection and therefore live in moist, shady areas.

The other group, TRACHEOPHYTA, are the vascular plants. The true stem is present in the lower ones from which evolved the true roots and leaves. Fern, club moss, horsetails, conifers, and flowering plants are all tracheophytes.

On the geological timetable embryophytes first appeared over 500 million years ago during the Silurian period in the Paleozoic Era. Fossils give evidence of seed ferns, horsetails, Lycopods, and the first forest plants. Angiosperms appeared about 200 million years ago during the Jurassic period in the Mesozoic Era. Cycads, conifers, and flowering plants grew with the dinosaurs. Today angiosperms are the world's dominant vegetation.   H.J.C.

SEE ALSO: ANGIOSPERMS; GYMNOSPERMS; PLANT TISSUES; PLANTS, CLASSIFICATION OF

A cut emerald gem

J. Daniel Willems

Emerald The emerald is a precious stone of a grassy green color. It is transparent, not brilliant or fiery. Its value depends on its color, size, and freedom from flaws.

Emerald is a form of BERYL, a silicate of aluminum and beryllium. The presence of CHROMIUM in the silicate causes the green color. Emerald is a soft stone, usually cut in a square or rectangular shape.

Emeralds are found in the Ural Mountains of Russia; in Colombia, South America; and in North Carolina. Fine emerald GEMS are more costly than fine diamonds.   C. L. K.

Emery see Corundum

Emphysema (em-fi-SEE-mah) There are several kinds of emphysema. The most important type affects the LUNGS. They become overly distended with air. A person with emphysema may be short of breath even at rest. The condition is seen most often in older people who smoke cigarettes.

Interlaced around the air sacs (alveoli) and throughout the lung tissue is a network of elastic fibers. These act like tiny rubber bands that stretch when one breathes in and shorten when one exhales. As a result of repeated bronchial infections from bacteria and viruses, irritation from tobacco smoke, air pollution, and chronic coughing, these fibers lose their elasticity. They no longer contract. The lungs blow up and old air is trapped. Fresh oxygen cannot move in nor can carbon dioxide be breathed off.   B. M. H.

Emu see Birds, flightless

Emulsion When oil and water are mixed together in such a way that the little droplets of oil cannot be seen in the liquid, the product is an emulsion. An emulsion may also be the opposite—droplets of water that are so well mixed into oil that they cannot be seen.

Homogenized MILK is a good example of an emulsion. The particles of cream are mixed into the milk to form the emulsion. Mayonnaise is emulsified, while vinegar-and-oil salad dressings are not. Some medicines, such as CASTOR OIL, are emulsified so they are more pleasant to taste.   J. D. B.

SEE ALSO: SOLUTION

Enamel see Paint, Teeth

Encyst see Parasites

✳ **THINGS TO DO**

WHAT IS AN EMULSION?

1   **Beat one teaspoon of vinegar and four teaspoons of salad oil together. Let them stand for a few minutes.**

2   **This is not an emulsion because the oil and vinegar separate.**

3   **Now beat an egg and a teaspoon of vinegar together. Add four teaspoons of oil and beat again.**

4   **This mixture is an emulsion. All the ingredients stay mixed together.**

                            J.D.B.

Endangered species Types of plants and animals currently threatened with EXTINCTION are called endangered species. Various organizations list thousands of different animals on their endangered lists. Some of the MAMMALIA in danger of dying out completely are bobcats, grizzly bears, cheetahs, Asian elephants, gorillas, leopards, Asian lions, giant pandas, tigers, and gray whales. Endangered REPTILIA include the American crocodile as well as the Indian python. Some endangered BIRDS are the bald eagle, the West African ostrich, the California condor, and the golden parakeet.

Animal species known to be endangered include more than five hundred mammals, over a thousand birds, over two thousand INVERTEBRATES, more than five hundred FISH, and about fifty amphibians. Many other animals are probably endangered but have not been identified. In order to survive, many well-known animal species may have to live entirely in captivity in zoos and nature preserves. Whether many species can survive this way for long is not known. Currently, efforts are being made to protect only a tiny fraction of the world's endangered animals and plants.

Including those yet to be discovered, there may be more endangered plants than animals. One branch of the government that tries to learn about some of them is the U.S. Fish and Wildlife Service. Its 1992 list of endangered plants included the Maguire daisy, Florida golden aster, Bakersfield cactus, Texas wild rice, and autumn buttercup.

Some scientists suspect that whole species of plants may be disappearing before they are even discovered and named. Destruction of the South American rain forest, for one example, is endangering many forms of plants (and animals) that live nowhere else.

The reasons plants and animals are in danger of extinction are numerous: loss of habitat, shortage of food, increase of predators, overpopulation of people, city sprawl, biocides, deforestation, excessive hunting, chemical pollution, and agricultural expansion.

One species of animals, the human race, is endangering millions of other species. This is a global problem in need of action now. J.H.

SEE ALSO: BALANCE OF NATURE, ECOLOGY, EXTINCTION, JUNGLE, INTERNATIONAL CONTROL OF NATURAL RESOURCES

Endive Endive is an Old World plant which has been grown for less than 2000 years. This herb is a salad green.

Endocrine glands (ENN-doh-krinn) Endocrine glands secrete HORMONES directly into the bloodstream.

SEE: ADRENAL GLANDS, OVARY, PANCREAS, PARATHYROID, PINEAL GLAND, PITUITARY GLAND, TESTES, THYMUS, THYROID

Endoderm Endoderm is the inner of the three primary germ layers formed during the early embryonic development of a multicellular animal. From it come the lining of most of the alimentary canal and the chief digestive organs.

SEE: CLEAVAGE, EMBRYOLOGY

Endoscope An endoscope is an instrument that allows visual examination of the inside of a hollow human organ.

Newer endoscopes are flexible, wire-like instruments with a light on the end. They are called *fiber-optic* endoscopes, and can be used to see the lining of the stomach or inside the bladder or *colon* (large intestine). They help doctors see inside without surgery. E.S.S.

Endoskeleton Endoskeleton is the internal SKELETON or supporting structure of bones and cartilage characteristic of the vertebrates. It includes the vertebral column, ribs, skull, and the pectoral and pelvic girdles.

Endothermic Endothermic is a term describing a chemical reaction in which HEAT is continuously absorbed and must be supplied to keep the reaction going. An example is the reaction of nitrogen and oxygen to form nitric oxide.

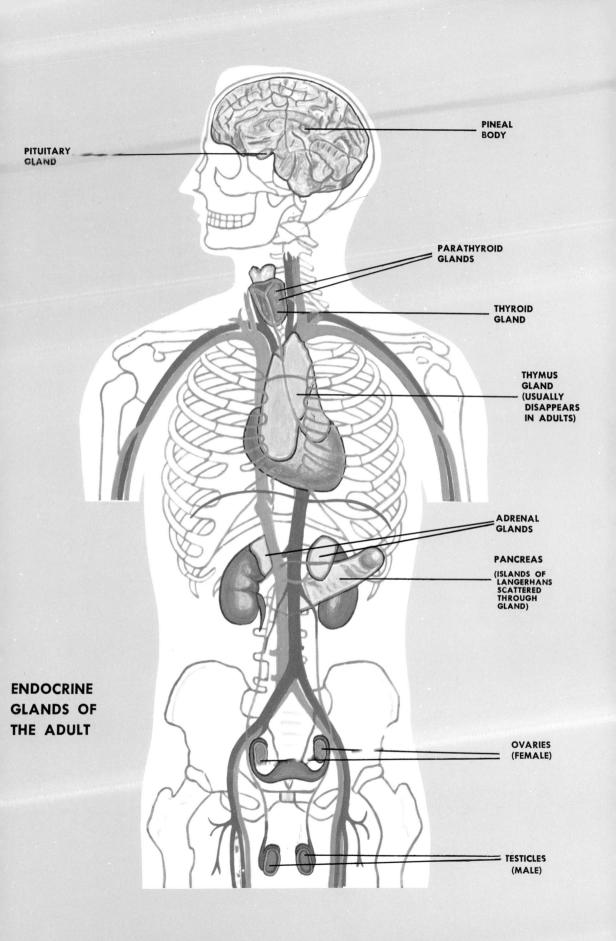

PITUITARY GLAND

PINEAL BODY

PARATHYROID GLANDS

THYROID GLAND

THYMUS GLAND (USUALLY DISAPPEARS IN ADULTS)

ADRENAL GLANDS

PANCREAS (ISLANDS OF LANGERHANS SCATTERED THROUGH GLAND)

ENDOCRINE GLANDS OF THE ADULT

OVARIES (FEMALE)

TESTICLES (MALE)

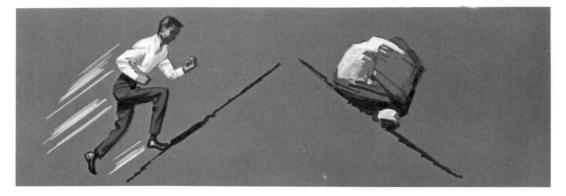

A boy running up the hill shows kinetic energy. The balanced rock, ready to roll, has potential energy

Energy Energy is the ability to do work. Energy is needed for a person to work, to jump, to run, to eat, and so forth. Energy is needed for plants and animals to grow. It is present in another form in the electricity that lights lamps and makes television sets produce pictures. Energy is in the coal or oil that is burned for fuel in furnaces and in the fuel used in the engines of cars and airplanes.

KINDS OF ENERGY

The chief forms of energy are: mechanical (and muscle), chemical, heat, nuclear, and energy of electromagnetic radiation. Besides these, there are other ways of classifying energy. For instance, it may be divided into two *action types*. One such type is *kinetic energy;* the other *potential energy*. Kinetic energy can be called "moving energy." Examples of this type are a boy running or water pouring down a waterfall. Potential energy is "stored" energy. It is that energy stored in a watch spring that is all coiled up or in a large stone just ready to drop from the top of a hill. Kinetic energy can then be described as the energy possessed by a system due to its *motion*. Potential energy is the energy possessed by a system or an object due to its *position*.

CONSERVATION OF ENERGY

Although one kind of energy may be converted easily into another, such as potential to kinetic type or chemical to electrical form, the total energy *always remains the same*. That is, energy is neither created nor destroyed in any given physical system. This idea is called the *law of conservation of energy*. Another way to state this idea is to say that for every quantity of energy of a given form that seems to disappear, the same amount of energy of some other form really appears, or the same total quantity of several forms (or types) appears. A further example is shown by the following: A bullet leaves a gun with a certain kinetic energy. As it flies through the air, some of its energy is lost or converted to heat energy due to its friction with the air. As the bullet strikes its target, more energy is converted to sound and light. Heat will also be developed in the target, while fragments of the bullet will carry away some energy. If all of these "pieces" of lost or converted energy are totalled, they will equal the original kinetic energy with which the bullet was fired.

According to EINSTEIN's theories, which are too complicated to detail here, there is also a relationship between matter and energy that deals with conservation of both. It is now known, by observing radioactive decomposition, that matter may also be converted to energy. An equation was created to show that this conversion takes place without loss:

$$E = mc^2$$

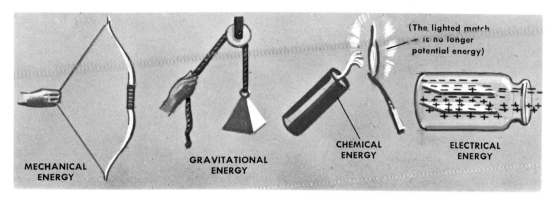

MECHANICAL ENERGY

GRAVITATIONAL ENERGY

CHEMICAL ENERGY

(The lighted match is no longer potential energy)

ELECTRICAL ENERGY

Each of the forms of potential energy can instantly be converted to kinetic energy

where E, the energy, is equal to m, the mass or weight loss during the radioactive decomposition, multiplied by c^2, the speed of light squared.

THE HUMAN BODY AND ENERGY

The human body may be likened to a machine in its use of energy to perform its daily work. The energy for this work comes from CARBOHYDRATES, FATS, and PROTEINS, which are broken down in the body and their potential energy transferred. Some of the energy "captured" is used to do work inside the body and some of it is used to do work outside the body. This means that energy is needed for inside work, such as pumping blood, while a good portion of that energy is needed for doing outside work, such as walking, carrying packages, and climbing stairs. The conservation law also seems to hold true for the body. If a person were to spend a day in a controlled room, it could be proved that the energy in the food eaten would be converted to an equal amount of heat energy, due to the internal and external work done by the person.

POTENTIAL AND KINETIC ENERGY

In order to be of some use, potential energy must be changed into kinetic energy. Water flowing over the edge of a dam, for example, has its potential energy "built-in" by the fact that work was necessary to lift it to the top of the dam. As the water flows over the top, its potential energy is being changed to kinetic energy. By the time it reaches the river below, all the potential energy is changed to kinetic. At any time in between the top and the bottom, however, the sum of the two energies is always equal to the total potential energy at the start, which is in turn equal to the kinetic energy at the end.

CONSERVATION OF ENERGY

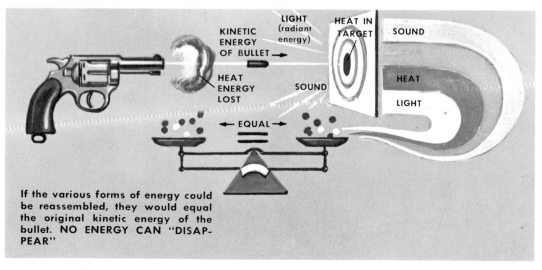

KINETIC ENERGY OF BULLET →

HEAT ENERGY LOST

LIGHT (radiant energy)

HEAT IN TARGET

SOUND

SOUND

HEAT

LIGHT

← EQUAL →

If the various forms of energy could be reassembled, they would equal the original kinetic energy of the bullet. **NO ENERGY CAN "DISAPPEAR"**

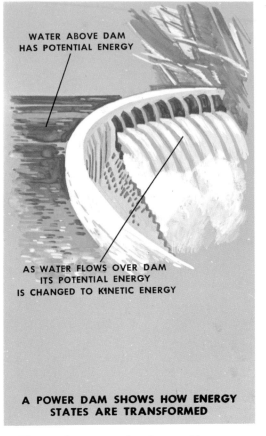

WATER ABOVE DAM HAS POTENTIAL ENERGY

AS WATER FLOWS OVER DAM ITS POTENTIAL ENERGY IS CHANGED TO KINETIC ENERGY

A POWER DAM SHOWS HOW ENERGY STATES ARE TRANSFORMED

Water going over a dam has usable energy

Conversion of kinetic energy into potential can be illustrated by the WINDMILL. The kinetic energy of the wheel as it spins can lift water and store it in a tank. The work done in lifting the water is stored as potential energy in the water. If the water is allowed to fall back to earth, this potential energy is again converted to kinetic energy.

Potential energy of an elevated body may be calculated from the formula:

$$P.E. = mgh$$

where *P.E.*, the potential energy, is equal to *m*, the mass, multiplied by *g*, the acceleration due to gravity, multiplied by *h*, the vertical distance through which the mass is lifted. For kinetic energy, the following formula can be used:

$$K.E. = \tfrac{1}{2}mv^2$$

where *K.E.*, the kinetic energy, is equal to $\tfrac{1}{2}m$, the mass, multiplied by v^2, the square of the speed at which the mass is moving. The units of measurement used in the above formulas are shown in the table at the top of the next column.

	English System	Metric System
K.E., *P.E.*	foot-poundals	joules
m	pounds	kilograms
g	feet per second per second	meters per second per second
h	feet	meters
v	feet per second	meters per second

CHEMICAL AND ELECTRICAL ENERGY

In the transforming of chemical energy into electrical energy, certain chemical reactions involve parts of the atoms of the elements in chemicals known as ELECTRONS. When these electrons are transferred from one chemical to another, an electric current can be set up. As an example, if two metal bars, such as zinc and copper, are partially immersed in a sulfuric acid solution, a chemical reaction takes place. If the parts of these bars that are above the surface of the acid solution are connected to each other by a wire, it will be found that an electric current will flow through this wire. This conversion of chemical energy to electrical energy was discovered by VOLTA. This conversion system is today called the *voltaic cell*, in his honor. Modifications of this simple system are used as batteries in automobiles, flashlights, and many other places where ELECTRICITY is necessary and cannot be obtained from a main line.

The wheel's kinetic energy lifts water to the tank. The water then has potential energy

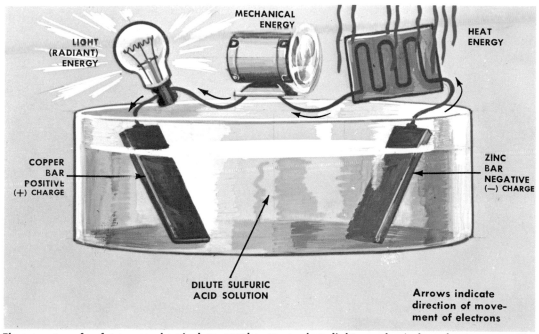

LIGHT (RADIANT) ENERGY

MECHANICAL ENERGY

HEAT ENERGY

COPPER BAR POSITIVE (+) CHARGE

ZINC BAR NEGATIVE (—) CHARGE

DILUTE SULFURIC ACID SOLUTION

Arrows indicate direction of movement of electrons

Electrons transfer from one chemical to another to produce light, mechanical, or heat energy. The energy conversion making this possible was discovered by Count Alessandro Volta

Electricity is purchased from the local electric company as electric energy. As shown above, the JOULE is the unit of energy. The term WATT is a unit of power. This unit is used to rate light bulbs according to the amount of power they use. The watt means that one joule of energy per second is being used up. The KILOWATT-HOUR is also a unit of energy derived from the equation:

$$energy = power \times time$$

The kilowatt-hour is the unit used in calculating an electric bill.

Another form of electric energy is the familiar radio wave. This energy is transmitted from antennas into space and picked up by RADIO receivers.

HEAT ENERGY

Heat energy is also obtained through the conversion of other sources of energy. The SUN is the earth's main source of surface heat energy. Its energy stems from nuclear fusion reactions occurring on its surface. These, of course, involve nuclear energy converting to heat energy. Another source of heat energy comes from geysers and volcanoes below the earth's surface. Energy in the form of heat that is derived from chemical reactions is well known in the fuels used to heat homes and run automobiles. Mechanical energy also can produce heat when it runs into difficulties in the form of FRICTION. Electrical energy produces heat for toasters, irons, heating pads, and other appliances.

NUCLEAR ENERGY

Since the end of World War II, NUCLEAR ENERGY has become an important and controversial source of energy for generating electric power. Nuclear fuel suitable for power plants can cost as little as half the price of FOSSIL FUELS such as PETROLEUM and COAL. At the start of 1992, 420 nuclear power plants were in operation worldwide. More than half of all the electric power produced in Belgium, France, and Sweden currently comes from nuclear energy.

Today, only Japan and France have aggressive programs to develop new nuclear power plants. In the U.S., which led the world with a total of 111 nuclear power stations at the start of 1992, there has not been a single order for a new nuclear plant since the 1970s. The decline in the U.S. and elsewhere is the result of concerns about accidents in operating plants and the safe disposal of waste material that can remain deadly for thousands of years.

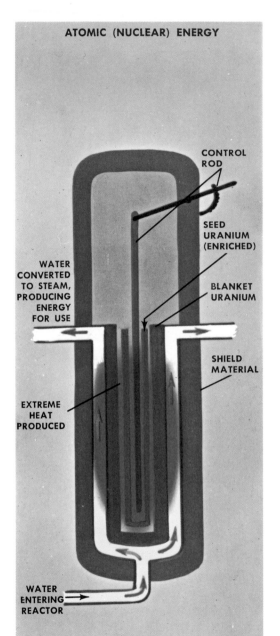

ATOMIC (NUCLEAR) ENERGY

CONTROL ROD

SEED URANIUM (ENRICHED)

WATER CONVERTED TO STEAM, PRODUCING ENERGY FOR USE

BLANKET URANIUM

SHIELD MATERIAL

EXTREME HEAT PRODUCED

WATER ENTERING REACTOR

Great amounts of energy are produced by the fission (splitting of the nucleus) of atoms. Above is a diagram of a thermal nuclear reactor of the pressurized water type. Hot water under pressure enters the reactor; the fission of uranium atoms then produces so much heat that water is changed to steam. This is done in the coils of a heat exchanger (not shown). The steam drives turbines or other machinery. The control rod is made of cadmium, or some similar element. It absorbs the neutrons of atomic nuclei without itself being changed. Therefore, it is used to slow down, or speed up, the reaction

TRANSFER OF ENERGY

There are several ways in which energy can be moved along a given course. Electrical energy is moved through a wire by means of electrons. Heat energy is transferred from a bowl of hot soup through a spoon out to the end of its handle by the motion of invisible molecules of the metal in the spoon. The wind can transfer its energy to a lake, filling it full of rough waves. The sun's energy and electrical energy, in the form of radio waves, are also carried along by waves. These forms of energy cannot be seen, heard, or felt until they reach their destination and change forms.

Just as the various forms of energy can be converted to heat energy, heat itself can be converted to other forms of energy. When gasoline is burned in an automobile ENGINE, for example, the heat energy is changed to mechanical energy to work the pistons and crankshaft. The heat energy of every single thing in the universe is constantly being converted to radiant energy and eventually being lost to outer space. Heat energy is not a measurement of temperature alone, but also depends upon the amount of material present. As an example, a full cup of water at a temperature of 100° F. (37.8° C.) will have twice the heat energy of half a cup at the same temperature. Heat energy can be transferred easily from one object to another in any one of three different ways. These three ways of transferring heat are called conduction, convection, and radiation. *Conduction* of heat works through direct contact of the heat source and the body accepting the heat. CONVECTION of heat energy takes place by the actual movement of a heated liquid or gas, such as air. The heated liquid or gas then makes contact with the object accepting the heat. The third transfer process is called RADIATION, which does not use direct contact in order to transfer heat energy. Radiant energy, such as that from the sun, travels through empty space at 186,000 miles (300,000 kilometers) per second. When the rays strike an object, this energy is again converted to heat energy.

ENERGY AND WORK

Count Rumford (Benjamin Thompson) is considered to be the discoverer of the relationship between heat energy and work. Thompson found that large amounts of heat

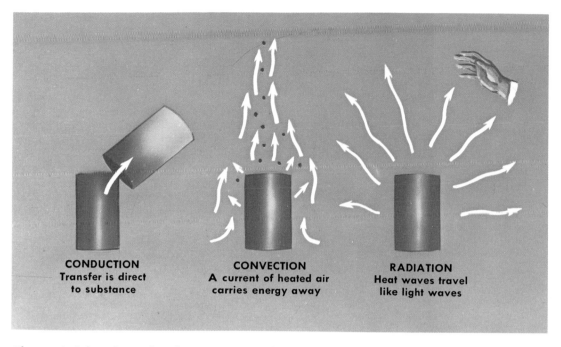

CONDUCTION
Transfer is direct
to substance

CONVECTION
A current of heated air
carries energy away

RADIATION
Heat waves travel
like light waves

These principles of transfer of energy are used daily in most homes. Food is cooked by conduction, refrigeration is obtained by convection and homes are heated by radiation

were developed in the boring of holes to make cannons. This type of work was done with horses and it involved a great deal of friction. Thompson found that the faster the horses were made to work, that is the more energy they used, the more heat was developed in the particles of metal that were being bored out. He was able to demonstrate this by putting these particles in water and observing the temperature rise in the water with a thermometer. It was shown that the more energy the horses used, the higher the temperature of the water rose from the metal particles, or the more heat energy was developed.

James Prescott Joule was able to refine this system, making it extremely accurate. The unit of work, the joule, is named for him. He was able to find an exact mechanical or work term for heat. The following equations show these relationships for the two common systems of measurement:

4.18 joules = 1 calorie;

778 foot-pounds of work = 1 BRITISH THERMAL UNIT or B.T.U.   M.S.

SEE ALSO: CALORIE; HEAT; JOULE; MACHINES, SIMPLE; POWER; WORK

Energy conversion see Energy, Machinery

Energy crisis Energy crisis refers to concerns that FOSSIL FUELS such as PETROLEUM, NATURAL GAS, and COAL will soon be used up and unavailable to meet future energy needs. Decades ago, during the 1970s, the term was used during a petroleum shortage.

In 1973, nations belonging to the Organization of Petroleum Exporting Countries (OPEC) created an energy crisis by cutting back their production of petroleum. At the same time, OPEC members drastically increased prices they charged for oil produced in their lands. As a result of OPEC's tactics, oil supplies throughout much of the world dwindled and long lines at automotive gasoline stations developed in many different countries. Over the next few decades, prices for petroleum fell, and supplies were plentiful, at least for the world's immediate needs. Talk of an "energy crisis" decreased. However, the supplies of

Some giant power plants use tremendous amounts of fossil fuels.

Solar energy is a possible alternative to using oil and coal as energy sources.

Commonwealth Edison

Argonne National Laboratories

WHAT CAN I DO ABOUT IT?

As both the world population and technology expand, there is increased demand on reserves of fossil fuels (coal, oil, and natural gas) for energy. We all need to reduce our energy usage to make convenient fuel deposits last as long as possible. Here are some ways we can help reserve fuel sources for ever increasing energy demands.

1. Turn off unnecessary lights and machines. (When less electricity is used, power companies will use less fuel.)

2. Raise thermostat settings in summer to 78° F (26° C) or above and lower winter settings to 65° F (18° C) or below. (This will result in less fuel use.)

3. Improve building construction with insulation to keep buildings cooler in summer and warmer in winter. (This will reduce use of energy for heating and cooling.)

4. Take short showers; run washing machines only when full. (Fuel is used to heat water. Using less hot water is using less energy.)

5. Recycle paper, aluminum, glass and plastic. (It takes less energy to process recycled goods than to produce goods from raw materials.)

6. Use public transportation, drive smaller cars or form car pools. (Smaller cars burn less fuel; traveling together reduces the number of vehicles burning fuel.)

7. Obey speed limits when driving. (Lower limits reduce accident rates and also increase mileage—meaning less fuel usage.)

fossil fuels are limited. An energy crisis may develop again.

In 1991, the Congressional Research Service of the U.S. Library of Congress conducted a major study of world petroleum needs and supplies. The study showed that if petroleum was evenly distributed around the world, and if demand remained at 1991 levels, known supplies and suspected new sources of crude petroleum would be adequate until sometime in the middle of the twenty-first century. Demand for petroleum is likely to increase, however, and remaining crude petroleum is very unevenly spread around the world. Approximately half of the crude petroleum known to still exist underground is located in the area of the Persian Gulf. Most of it is controlled by the Organization of Petroleum Exporting Countries. The 1991 Persian Gulf War is an example of oil-related disputes that may increase as supplies are

consumed and nations are increasingly dependent on oil from the Persian Gulf region.

Supplies of another fossil fuel, natural gas, may be even more limited than crude petroleum. Concerns that natural gas shortages may begin as early as the end of the twentieth century have increased efforts to develop new sources. One of the most promising new technologies involves transforming a form of highly polluting coal into clean-burning gas in a process called *coal gasification*.

Many of the efforts to diminish the possibility of a future energy crisis developing center around conservation of existing supplies. New forms of renewable energy, such as solar, wind, and GEOTHERMAL ENERGY, are being explored for possible practical applications. NUCLEAR ENERGY, if operational and waste-disposal safety concerns are satisfied, also offers hope.   J.H.

SEE ALSO: ENERGY, FUEL, SOLAR CELL, WINDMILL

Engine

Engine An engine is a machine which changes ENERGY into some form of useful mechanical work. At one time, wind machines (windmills) and water-powered machines (waterwheels) were broadly classified as engines. Today the term *engine* refers to the *external-* or *internal*-combustion engines. These engines transform the *potential* energy of heat (thermal energy) into mechanical work. The wind and waterpower devices depend upon the *kinetic* energy of blowing wind or falling water to produce useful work.

The steam or gas TURBINE performs a function similar to the engine but uses both potential and kinetic energies to accomplish useful work. Steam, at very high temperatures and pressures, is used to spin a turbine wheel to drive electric generators and to propel ships. Gas driven turbines supply power for airplanes and automobiles.

EXTERNAL-COMBUSTION

External-combustion engines use three separate units to produce power. The first is a *furnace* that burns a fuel, such as coal, oil, or gas. This fuel heats water in a *boiler,* the second unit. Water is heated to the boiling point when steam begins to form, and is then heated to higher temperatures to produce *superheated* steam at high pressures. This high pressure steam is piped to the third unit, a turbine or a *reciprocating* engine.

Before describing the action of the reciprocating engine, it must be mentioned that in some of the most modern power-producing systems, the furnace is not limited to a coal, oil, or gas burning unit. These more recent furnaces may use *solar* energy, or NU-

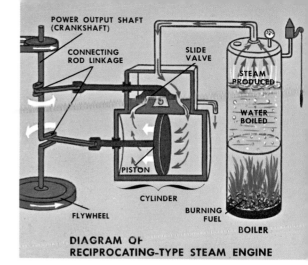

DIAGRAM OF RECIPROCATING-TYPE STEAM ENGINE

The early steam engines, though inefficient, opened the way to modern industry

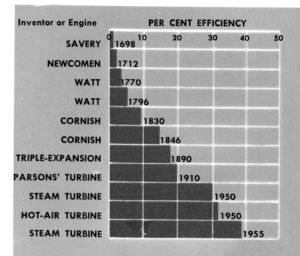

Inventor or Engine	PER CENT EFFICIENCY
	0 10 20 30 40 50
SAVERY	1698
NEWCOMEN	1712
WATT	1770
WATT	1796
CORNISH	1830
CORNISH	1846
TRIPLE-EXPANSION	1890
PARSONS' TURBINE	1910
STEAM TURBINE	1950
HOT-AIR TURBINE	1950
STEAM TURBINE	1955

The giant, triple-flow steam turbine is used to produce great quantities of power

Allis-Chalmers Mfg. Co.

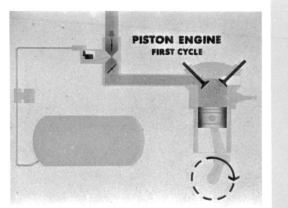

PISTON ENGINE FIRST CYCLE

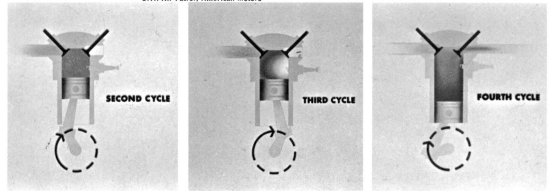

The four cycles of the piston engine (right) are intake, compression, explosion, exhaust

Civil Air Patrol; American Motors

SECOND CYCLE

THIRD CYCLE

FOURTH CYCLE

CLEAR ENERGY. Solar energy is derived from the heat of the sun, and it may come directly from the sun's rays or be stored for later use. Nuclear energy results from the intense heat given off when the uranium atom is split in an atomic reactor. This type of reaction is known as fission.

A simple reciprocating engine consists of a *cylinder* in which the piston moves when high pressure steam from the boiler rushes into the cylinder through properly timed *inlet* valves. A *connecting rod* connects the piston to a *crankshaft* which, in turn, rotates a *flywheel* and the engine *drive shaft*. The momentum of the flywheel moves the piston in the cylinder sufficiently to uncover the inlet valve to permit the rush of steam for the next cycle. The steam not used is pushed out of the cylinder through the *exhaust* valves. The working power of the engine is taken off at the drive shaft. Its amount depends upon the quantity and pressure of the steam delivered to the cylinder. This power may drive machinery such as generators, pumps, hoists, drop hammers, and drilling rigs.

Reciprocating steam engines are classified in several ways:

(1) *by action:* (a) single acting—steam is admitted at one end of the cylinder; (b) double acting—steam is admitted alternately at both ends of the cylinder;

(2) *by direction of piston movement:* (a) horizontal; (b) vertical; (c) inclined;

(3) *by stages of expansion:* (a) double—a larger cylinder further expands steam from the first cylinder; (b) triple—a larger cylinder further expands steam from the second cylinder;

(4) *by steam entry and exhaust position:* (a) counterflow—steam enters and leaves at the same end of the cylinder; (b) uniflow—steam enters at the end, and leaves (exhausts) at the middle of the cylinder.

The valve mechanism is the most critical part of the engine. The maximum power produced depends upon how well the valve admits steam, seals the cylinder during steam expansion, and exhausts the steam. An example was given of the sliding valve used in a simple engine. Lifting type valves are used for very high-temperature steam closures. These are disk-shaped valves which raise and lower from ports in the cylinder head.

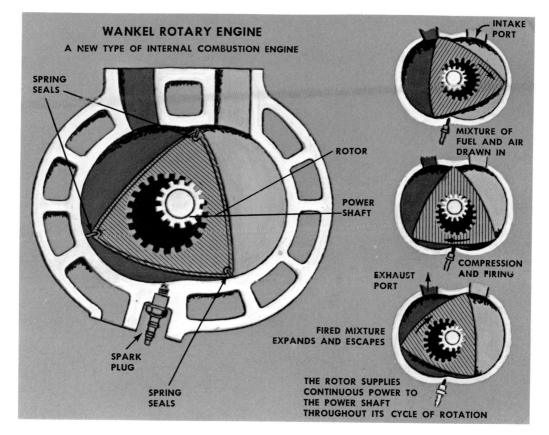

WANKEL ROTARY ENGINE
A NEW TYPE OF INTERNAL COMBUSTION ENGINE

SPRING SEALS

ROTOR

POWER SHAFT

SPARK PLUG

SPRING SEALS

INTAKE PORT

MIXTURE OF FUEL AND AIR DRAWN IN

COMPRESSION AND FIRING

EXHAUST PORT

FIRED MIXTURE EXPANDS AND ESCAPES

THE ROTOR SUPPLIES CONTINUOUS POWER TO THE POWER SHAFT THROUGHOUT ITS CYCLE OF ROTATION

Steam engines have high rotational energy (torque) and variable speed, both desirable traits for operating heavy machinery. However, because of higher operating costs, steam locomotives have been replaced by *diesel* power. Likewise, steam turbines are preferred to piston engines for propelling ships. Power of reciprocating steam engines does not exceed 1,000 h.p., whereas steam turbines develop many times that amount.

INTERNAL-COMBUSTION

The internal-combustion engine differs from the external-combustion in that the fuel is burned rapidly within the engine. The basic operations of this engine are like a reciprocating steam engine, regardless of whether the internal-combustion is a reciprocating or turbine engine. There are modifications due to the different fuels used. All internal-combustion engines have a characteristic cycle: (1) air and fuel are compressed; (2) fuel combustion under high compression makes high temperatures to produce work;

(3) the heated gases expand back to normal pressures; and (4) the gases that remain represent used products of combustion and are removed through a suitable arrangement of exhaust valves or ports.

A. *Reciprocating:* gasoline and diesel engines are the common reciprocating internal-combustion engines. The major difference between these engines is that the gasoline engine burns fuel at constant *volume,* called the *Otto cycle,* while the diesel burns fuel at constant *pressure,* called the *diesel cycle.*

1. *Gasoline reciprocating engines:* Gasoline piston-type engines are commonly used as power sources for automobiles, trucks, aircraft, boats, lawn mowers and many other powered devices. The smaller utility engines produce as little as one HORSEPOWER, while the larger aircraft engines exceed 3000 horsepower.

Characteristic of the gasoline engine is a *carburetor* for feeding the fuel and mixing it with air outside the combustion chamber; and an *ignition system* for firing the mixture.

Although gasoline engines may assume several different shapes due to the arrangement of cylinders (in a line, "V", horizontally opposed, and radial), they basically function as either a two-stroke cycle or four-stroke cycle engine.

The two-stroke engine requires two strokes of the piston (one revolution of the crankshaft) to complete the combustion cycle, while the four-stroke engine requires four strokes of the piston (two revolutions of the crankshaft) to complete its cycle.

a) *Four-stroke:* On the first stroke down, the air and fuel vapor are admitted to the cylinder by opening the intake valve. During the second stroke, the intake valve closes and compression starts. At the start of the third stroke (the power stroke), an electric discharge from the spark plug ignites the fuel mixture causing a mild explosion. This explosion makes the expanding gases push the piston downward. The fourth stroke completes the cycle by opening the exhaust valve to release the burned gases from the cylinder.

A battery-powered starting motor is commonly used to revolve the crankshaft initially. The intake and exhaust valves are geared to the crankshaft to coordinate their proper opening and closing.

The four-stroke automotive engine has a power stroke only once in four strokes

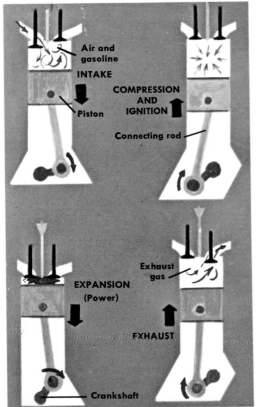

A TWO-CYCLE INTERNAL COMBUSTION ENGINE

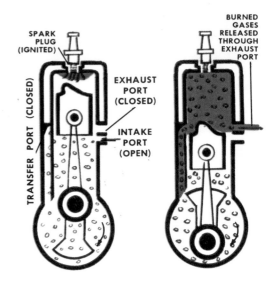

The two-stroke engine has a power stroke every other stroke

b) *Two-stroke:* A similar operation takes place in the two-stroke cycle, except the valves are replaced by ports in the cylinder walls which are uncovered as the piston passes by. During the first stroke, the fuel mixture enters the cylinder and is compressed. The fuel mixture is ignited at the start of the second stroke, while the burned gases are exhausted at the end of the stroke.

It would seem logical that since the two-stroke engine has a power stroke twice as often as the four-stroke engine, the power developed by the two-stroke engine would be twice that of the four-stroke engine. But, because of the less efficient removal of the fuel and gases through the exhaust port, the two-stroke engine develops only 70-90 percent more horsepower than a four-stroke engine of similar size.

2. *Diesel:* The characteristic difference in operation between the gasoline engine and diesel engine is that the diesel admits only air during the intake stroke, and the diesel fuel is automatically ignited when forced into the cylinder. The diesel engine, therefore, has no carburetor or ignition system. The diesel fuel is injected into the combustion chamber under high pressure. An air COMPRESSOR is used to give the diesel

engine its first revolution. As the fine spray of fuel thoroughly intermixes with the highly compressed, high-temperature air, combustion occurs. Fuel injection, ignition, and combustion all take place within a few thousandths of a second.

The high compression of the diesel cycle makes possible the use of low-cost, low-grade oils as fuel. This, with the high heat efficiency, makes the diesel practical for train locomotives, trucks, small electric generators, and large pumps. Horsepowers range from 50 to 5,000.

B. *Other Internal-Combustion Engines:* In addition to the reciprocating piston internal combustion engines, there are rotary types such as the *gas turbine* and *Wankel* engine, both illustrated here.

A simple gas turbine consists of (a) a rotary compressor unit; (b) a combustion chamber; and (c) a turbine. For operation details, see TURBINE.

The most familiar application of the gas turbine is the *turbojet* engine used by aircraft. Here heated gases directed at turbine blades cause the turbine to rotate 8,000–16,000 revolutions per minute. The gases are forced out through a nozzle at high velocity to produce the action-reaction *thrust* required for propulsion. A variation of this

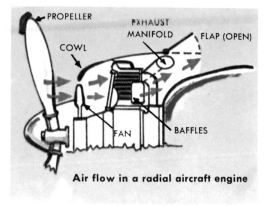

Air flow in a radial aircraft engine

application is the *turboprop*. In this the turbine drives a propeller, which produces 80 percent of the aircraft's power, while the jet thrust provides the other 20 percent.

Advantages of the turbine engine are: except for a starter plug, no ignition system is needed; no pistons or valves are used; there is little or no vibration; and the engine is self-cooling. Turbine horsepower-to-weight ratios are higher than for any other engine. However, turbines do have high fuel consumption per horsepower developed.　　H. P. O.

SEE ALSO: AUTOMOBILE, JET PROPULSION, MOTOR, NUCLEAR ENERGY, ROCKET ENGINE, STEAM

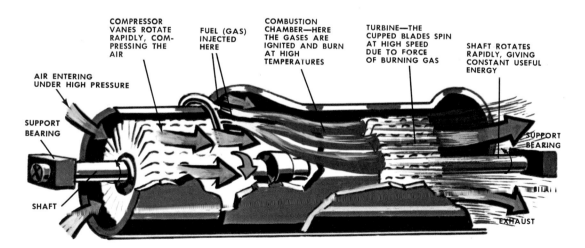

SINGLE-SHAFT GAS TURBINE ENGINE

This type of engine is used in stationary power plants

A gas turbine has one main rotating shaft running down its core. The great efficiency of this type of engine is due to the rapid conversion of heat energy to kinetic energy in the turbine. Also, the motion of the shaft is smooth and continuous, rather than "up and down" as in a piston engine. There is no power lost.

Modern architectural engineering has made possible the building of tall skyscrapers. The Sears Tower (center building) in Chicago, Illinois, is the tallest structure in the world, rising 110 stories or 1,454 feet (443 meters) above the city. Two radio antennas bring its total height to 1,800 feet (549 meters).

Engineering Engineering may be defined as that branch of learning that concerns itself with the conversion and application of the materials and forces of nature to the purposes of man. The one who practices engineering, the *engineer,* is not ordinarily a scientist because a scientist is an experimenter and discoverer. The engineer uses the materials and ENERGY that have been discovered by the scientist to adapt them to a useful result.

The results achieved by the engineer may be the use of a material such as stone, concrete, glass, or steel to form a building, a dam, or a highway. The result may also be the harnessing of some form of energy such as electricity, the steam in a boiler, the explosive energy of gasoline or TNT, or even the tremendous force of a smashed atom.

The engineer must be analytical, creative, and inventive. He is always looking for a better way—newer, cheaper, and more productive uses of the resources of materials and energy to improve man's standard of living.

HISTORY

Great engineering marvels have been traced back to Biblical times. The Pyramids of Egypt stand even today, but the Hanging Gardens of Babylon have long since disappeared. The harbors built by the ancient Greeks, and the roads, bridges, aqueducts, and drainage systems constructed by the Romans, are later examples of magnificent engineering achievement. Calling those who originated these projects "engineers" has led to some dispute. Who could say those builders understood the basic reasons for the success of their accomplishments? Some argue that it was not by analysis or by formula that they were able to predict the results, but by trial and error. Nevertheless, modern engineering feats are still rivaled by the skill of past master builders.

McDonnell-Douglas Corp

Aeronautical engineers use wind tunnels to stress test airplane designs.

Two main divisions of engineering are noted for historical purposes. The first is the field of *military engineering* which developed ballistics, and war machines such as catapults and wall-scaling devices. As man realized the benefits of military engineering in war, he turned toward peaceful application of the science. Thus out of military engineering grew the second division, *civil engineering*. This field was called "civil" to separate it from military applications.

The modern development of civil engineering began in the 18th century with the construction of canals, roads and bridges—the most outstanding advance since before the Dark Ages. John Smeaton (1724–1792) was the first to be given recognition as a civil engineer. The United States Military Academy at West Point offered the first general engineering course in this country in 1802, while Rensselaer Polytechnic Institute at Troy, New York, offered the first civil engineering degree in 1824. As the need developed for engineers to exchange their ideas, the American Society of Civil Engineers was founded in 1852.

Several inventions in the 19th century complicated the existing field of civil engineering so that it became necessary to branch into different fields. This period of mechanical development, which brought forth the steam engine, the cotton gin, and the spinning jenny, contributed to the beginnings of mechanical engineering; while civil engineering became involved only with surveying, mapping, and the construction of bridges, roads, and buildings. From this period on, engineering grew rapidly, expanding and specializing in new fields.

FIELDS OF ENGINEERING

The Engineers' Council of Professional Development (E.C.P.D.), a government agency, establishes the educational and professional standards of engineering. It also gives accreditation to many branches of engineering which include the following:

Aeronautical (including Aerospace)	Mechanical
	Metallurgical
Agricultural	Mining
Architectural	Naval and Marine
Ceramic	Nuclear
Chemical	Petroleum
Civil	Sanitary (including Municipal)
Electrical (including Electronic)	
	Textile
Industrial	Transportation

It will be appreciated that the above listing of accredited engineering courses of study does not include many of the specialized fields of engineering. This is because they are closely associated with other engineering classifications. Examples would be: welding engineering, closely associated with metallurgical engineering; hydraulic engineering as a branch of civil engineering; the relationship of automotive engineering with mechanical engineering; and the place occupied by astronautical engineering in the aerospace field.

EDUCATION IN ENGINEERING

The fundamental education of an engineer begins with extensive study in several physical sciences: MATHEMATICS, PHYSICS, CHEMISTRY, and MECHANICS. As an engineer specializes, he or she draws on those sciences which are the basis of their chosen field, such as biology, geology, or economics. Engineering courses accredited by E.C.P.D. require four or five years of study to obtain an undergraduate degree. An engineer can then study for a master's degree (one to two additional years), and then on to a doctor's degree (two years or more beyond the master's).

There are over 250 colleges and universities in the United States that award degrees in engineering. Graduates may take their place in the field, or go on to a higher level of study in engineering, medicine, or law.

MAIN ENGINEERING FIELDS

Of the many branches of engineering, there are some that are of particular importance in view of the technological advances that characterize the age we live in. These will be described briefly.

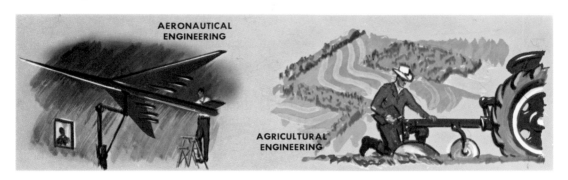

Aeronautical engineering: This branch of engineering is concerned with design, production, maintenance, and use of AIRCRAFT structures and power units. When aviation came into general use, its technical problems grew. Up until World War II, the aeronautical engineer could work on almost any phase of flight, whether it be operational or structural. However, recent years have seen the advent of jet propulsion, supersonic flight, missiles, rockets, satellites, and travel into outer space. All of these have added to the scope and importance of the aeronautical engineer, and even made necessary the development of an entirely new but related branch of engineering, *aerospace* engineering. With the apparently limitless range of outer space travel, another wide field of study and achievement has developed which is both a science and an engineering branch, the field of astronautics.

Agricultural engineering: The agricultural engineer is concerned with the physical problems in the preparation and production of land and in the storing and processing of agricultural products. Specialties include the use and operation of power and farm machinery, farm structures, and soil and water conservation. The agricultural engineer must have a thorough understanding of all phases of farming in addition to basic engineering.

Architectural engineering: Architectural engineering combines architecture with the structural design aspect of civil engineering for design and construction of buildings. An architect is concerned primarily with the appearance of his design, while the civil engineer regards structural soundness as his objective. By uniting the two fields, functional structures can be erected at a minimum cost. Structural, mechanical, and electrical systems are coordinated by the architectural engineer in all phases of building construction. The latest example of architectural engineering is the Sears Tower in Chicago, Illinois. It is the tallest building in the world.

Ceramic engineering: The ceramic engineer is concerned with the design and production of products made from nonmetallic, inorganic sands or clays. In addition to solving problems of brick, tile, and glass production, the ceramic engineer helps the electrical engineer with insulator problems and the missile engineer with heat and friction problems. Together with metallurgical engineers, the ceramic engineers developed a ceramic and metal mixture, called *cermet* which is superior to either individual ingredient for specific applications.

Chemical engineering: Using CHEMISTRY as his "pure science" foundation, the chemi-

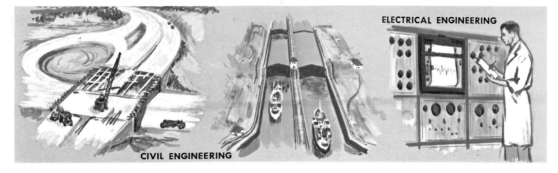

ELECTRICAL ENGINEERING

CIVIL ENGINEERING

cal engineer is most concerned with manufacturing processes where materials are changed in state, energy content, or composition. For example, chemical engineers devise the necessary equipment and methods for making rayon, nylon, explosives, drugs, petroleum products, plastics, and detergents, —to mention only a few. Engineers may also work in the laboratory controlling the operations and testing the products. While the chemist researches for new materials, the chemical engineer looks for ways to produce the materials quickly and cheaply.

Civil engineering: Civil engineers survey the lands to chart all areas of the civilized world; they also plan the construction of fixed structures and surface and underground transportation systems. This is, perhaps, the broadest of the engineering fields since many specialties evolve from it such as structural, highway, and hydraulic engineering; dam building; city planning; and bridge building. Most noteworthy of the accomplishments of the civil engineer are the Panama Canal, the Hoover and Grand Coulee dams, and the Golden Gate and Verrazano-Narrows bridges.

Electrical engineering: This branch of engineering deals with problems of ELECTRICITY and magnetism. The electrical engineer designs and tests generators, motors, transformers, and electrical appliances. He may be responsible for the installation of power lines. From this field has evolved the electronics, communications, and signal engineer. The greatest accomplishments of this branch include

ELECTRONICS, and the development of television, computers, control devices, transistors, and miniature integrated circuits.

Industrial engineering: Industrial engineering is concerned with the design, improvement and installation of combined systems of men, materials and equipment. This field is often thought of as management engineering for it covers a broad area of every manufacturing activity. The industrial engineer is involved with design, specification and evaluation of plant layouts, materials handling systems, methods analyses, wage systems, work measurement, and management operations in order to promote the most efficient organization practicable.

Mechanical engineering: This field treats the design, manufacture, and operation of machinery, engines and tools; and heating, refrigeration and ventilating equipment. The field is so broad that the engineer often specializes as a machine design, automotive, marine, power plant or heating and ventilating engineer. Most inventions have originated in the field of mechanical engineering.

Metallurgical engineering: The metallurgical engineer is interested in the practical use of the properties of METALS and their ALLOYS. He is involved in problems of extracting metals from their ores and of metal refining. The art of welding and heat treating are important advances in this field. The metallurgical engineer's specialized knowledge of metal characteristics has been important in enabling the United States to adapt materials to the rigors of outer space.

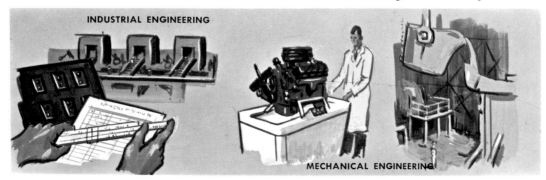

INDUSTRIAL ENGINEERING

MECHANICAL ENGINEERING

Mining engineering: This branch includes the location, design, and operation of mineral extractions from the earth. Prospecting for mine locations involves unique underground surveying. Ore transporting and handling techniques have become major engineering specialties within this field. Other allied fields have developed, directly or indirectly, such as petroleum, geological (earth's crust), and geophysical (earth's subsurface) engineering.

Nuclear engineering: As man has learned to split the atom and utilize its tremendous power, the need for this new branch of engineering developed. Starting with the development of Enrico Fermi's atomic chain reaction at the University of Chicago in 1942, the military and peaceful uses of atomic energy developed rapidly. Such problems as the control of the excessive temperatures and pressures of atomic fission, as well as those of radiation, had to be solved in order to harness atomic power. This became the area for the work of the nuclear engineer. Beginning with the late 1950s, the use of atomic reactors for the development of electric power, the propulsion of merchant ships and submarines, and other purposes led to the belief that nuclear energy would be the leading power source in the years to come.

Sanitary engineering: As an outgrowth of the civil engineering field, the sanitary engineer's primary interest is that of protecting public health. He is responsible for conceiving, designing, appraising, directing and managing public health works and projects. Such projects include the treatment and distribution of water supplies; the collection, treatment and disposal of sewage; the control of water pollution; rodent control; food control; and air pollution. Sanitary engineering is an extremely important function in large cities where there is dense population.

CAREERS IN ENGINEERING

Approximately 1.85 million engineers were working in the U.S. in 1991, out of a total work force of nearly 117 million people. The number of women in the engineering field has been increasing steadily, but in 1991 female engineers were still outnumbered more than ten to one by males.

Because engineers are needed in many different fields, the type of work they do is very diverse. Some engineers spend virtually all of their time in a single office or factory. Others travel to different locations, perhaps where a building or a road is under construction. Because a great deal of money is needed to complete most of the projects engineers design, the engineering field is strongly affected by economic conditions. The end of the Cold War, for example, coupled with an economic recession, created less demand for engineers in the aerospace industry during the early 1990s. On the other hand, new road and bridge projects promised by President Bill Clinton may well create many civil engineering jobs in the U.S.

In the future, there should be strong new demands for engineers in fields related to environmentalism, energy, communications, and computer science. In these as well as more traditional fields, engineers need a great deal of education. Today, most engineering jobs require a bachelor's degree from a university. In some highly technical fields, advanced degrees are virtual necessities. Students studying to become engineers generally take courses emphasizing science and mathematics as well as courses in a specific engineering field. Most new types of technology create demands for engineers. H.P.O.

English Channel see Europe

Entomology (enn-tuh-MAHL-uh-jee) Entomology is the science which deals with all phases of insect study, including the classification of insects. Classification is complex because there are thousands of kinds of insects. The effect of insects on AGRICULTURE is also studied.

SEE: ANIMALS, CLASSIFICATION OF; INSECTA

Environment (enn-VYE-run-muhnt) Environment is the total of all the physical and biological factors surrounding and within an organism. Microenvironment is the total of these same factors operating at a microscopic or submicroscopic level. Internal environment is the operation of these factors within the body.

SEE ALSO: BALANCE OF NATURE, ECOLOGY, ECOSYSTEM

Enzymes (ENN-zymes) Enzymes are organic compounds. These compounds contain the element carbon. Enzymes are made in the cell and function as catalysts. A catalyst speeds up a chemical reaction without taking part in the reaction. It is neither changed in any way nor destroyed by the reaction taking place. Each enzyme may take care of only one reaction. There are many enzymes in a living cell because there are many chemical reactions taking place all the time. Without enzymes, the cell would not be able to work.

Enzymes are made of protein. They function within a very narrow range of acidity or alkalinity. Most of them work best when cell sap is almost neutral. A narrow range of temperature is also essential. Without enzymes, many reactions would require so much heat in order to take place that the cell would die. Other reactions would take place too slowly without them. An enzyme can catalyze a reaction in either direction. If an enzyme causes A and B to make C, it can also cause C to break down into A and B.

An enzyme is named by adding the letters "ase" to the name of the substance that it catalyzes. For example, if it catalyzes a reaction in which a fat is broken down, the first part of the name comes from the Greek word *lipos,* meaning fat, plus the ending "ase," or *lipase*.

No one really knows how enzymes act as catalysts. It is believed, however, that they fit into and temporarily combine with some part of the molecules (substrate) that are going to take part in the reaction to be catalyzed. This idea is called the lock-and-key theory. It is a possibility because molecules are three dimensional with atoms and groups of atoms projecting out, above, below, and to either side of a main carbon skeleton. An enzyme may bring the substrate molecules and the molecules with which they react into a close enough association for the reaction to take place. At its conclusion, the enzyme is freed in order to repeat the process.

Some of the first enzymes isolated from living tissues were the digestive enzymes.

✳ **THINGS TO DO**

WHAT DO THE ENZYMES DO IN THE STOMACH?

1 Break an egg and separate the yellow from the white. Pour just the white part of the egg into a test tube.
2 Hold the tube over a flame until the white is cooked. Mark the level of the egg in the test tube.
3 Lay it in a pan of water to which pepsin has been added.
4 After one day observe the results. Now carefully add a few drops of dilute hydrochloric acid to the water and pepsin solution.
5 Let it stand for a second day and observe the change.
6 Pepsin is an enzyme in the stomach that breaks down proteins into simpler materials. However, it is not effective unless hydrochloric acid is present.
7 The other enzyme in the stomach, rennin, may be added to a cup of milk. It curds the milk and prepares it for the action of other enzymes.

These catalyze reactions in which the food eaten is broken down into simpler compounds by the addition of water. This type of reaction is called *hydrolysis.* Enzymes digesting starches and sugars are called *carbohydrases.* Fat-digesting enzymes are *lipases* and those working upon proteins are *proteases.* Some of them were named before there were rules for naming enzymes and the original names have been retained. Trypsin, erepsin,

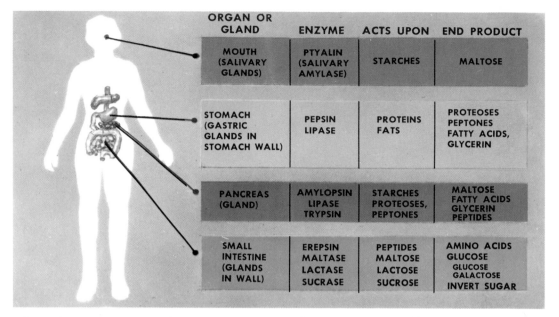

ORGAN OR GLAND	ENZYME	ACTS UPON	END PRODUCT
MOUTH (SALIVARY GLANDS)	PTYALIN (SALIVARY AMYLASE)	STARCHES	MALTOSE
STOMACH (GASTRIC GLANDS IN STOMACH WALL)	PEPSIN LIPASE	PROTEINS FATS	PROTEOSES PEPTONES FATTY ACIDS, GLYCERIN
PANCREAS (GLAND)	AMYLOPSIN LIPASE TRYPSIN	STARCHES PROTEOSES, PEPTONES	MALTOSE FATTY ACIDS GLYCERIN PEPTIDES
SMALL INTESTINE (GLANDS IN WALL)	EREPSIN MALTASE LACTASE SUCRASE	PEPTIDES MALTOSE LACTOSE SUCROSE	AMINO ACIDS GLUCOSE GLUCOSE GALACTOSE INVERT SUGAR

and pepsin are examples. They are all proteases.

Another whole group of enzymes catalyze the reactions involved in cellular respiration. Digested food is oxidized in cellular cytoplasm in order to release and store the energy necessary for the functioning of the cell. Waste products, carbon dioxide, and water are given off. (Oxidation is either the addition of oxygen to a substance or the removal of hydrogen from it.) There are more than 20 reactions involved in this process, and each of the reactions is controlled by an enzyme.

Enzymes are very important in inheritance. It is believed that GENES usually work by directing the formation of enzymes that catalyze reactions in which proteins are put together. These proteins may be such substances as eye pigments to give color to an eye, cellular bodies capable of secreting a specific substance, or hemoglobin for carrying oxygen in the blood stream. The actual gene is thought to be a variable number of sections called *nucleotides* of a DNA molecule. It is composed of a phosphate group from phosphoric acid, a five carbon sugar, and one of four organic bases.

Genes are very active during the embryology or development of an organism. Changes occurring between a single-celled zygote and a complex multicellular organism are often chemical ones, depending upon complex interactions between genes and the cellular environment and between different genes. As soon as the zygote becomes many celled, individual cells begin to occupy different environments. Inner cells, cut off from the outside and closed in on all sides by other cells, are different from outer cells. This leads to internal cellular differences in such factors as temperature, oxygen content, or acidity. Such changes affect the functioning of genes. Compounds developing in a group of cells may inhibit some of the genes. Also, compounds produced by action of one gene may be raw material for other genic action.   J. C. K.

SEE ALSO: ACIDS AND BASES, DIGESTIVE SYSTEM, ORGANIC COMPOUNDS, SUGARS

Eocene see Cenozoic Era, Geologic time table

Epidemic An epidemic is the sudden occurrence of an unusual number of cases of a contagious DISEASE in a community. Health officials keep records of reported cases of contagious diseases by day, week, month, and year. By comparison of such recorded data, health officers have an idea of the behavior of a contagious disease in a community. When the number of cases of a contagious disease is unusually high in comparison with the previous years, an epidemic exists. If several cases of a disease occur almost at the same time, it could be that they have a common source.

There are ways to detect the source of an epidemic. One way is to note the *incubation period* (the lapse of time between exposure to a disease and the first occurrence of symptoms). Health officers try to locate the source of a disease in an attempt to control the spread of it. They also must understand how contagious diseases are spread. Some are spread by coughing, by kissing, or by contaminating the water supply.

Epidemics occur in spurts. Chicken pox can be used as an example of the mechanism of an epidemic. In a given population many susceptible children can develop chicken pox. The rate can be so high that almost everyone in a certain age range becomes affected. After recovery from the attack, these patients become immune. The disease appears to die out temporarily in the community until a new generation of unprotected persons is born. Then, should an outsider bring a case to the community, a certain peak in the number of cases of chicken pox would appear which again could reach epidemic proportions.   G.A.D.

SEE ALSO: BLACK DEATH, MEDICINE

Epidermis see Skin

Epiglottis see Respiratory system

Epilepsy (EPP-uh-lepp-see) Epilepsy is a disease of the NERVOUS SYSTEM. It most commonly shows itself in sudden attacks of unconsciousness. No characteristic structural defect or injury of the BRAIN is found in all epileptics. In about 20% of all patients no brain change at all is detected. It can be diagnosed in the other 80% by the symptoms and by an abnormal brain wave test (ELECTROENCEPHALOGRAPH).

Along with unconsciousness, there are convulsive contractions of certain groups of muscles, which quickly spread to the whole body. These seizures are frequently preceded by certain sensations of the body so that the patient knows an attack is coming. The sensations, called the *aura*, vary widely. They may be a gripping sensation in the abdomen or a series of odd thoughts. The aura, as established by the individual patient, occurs before each attack.

Among the first groups of muscles that begin to have intermittent contractions are those of the head and jaws, followed by those of the limbs. If possible, a tape-wrapped tongue depressor is placed between the jaws to prevent the victim from biting his or her tongue. After moving a few minutes, the patient becomes quiet and remains unconscious for half an hour or more. This sequence is called a *seizure.*

There are three types of epilepsy. The severe type described above is called *grand mal;* a secondary, less dramatic type is called *petit mal.* The third type involves changes in mental activities. The patient remains consciousness, but there is a loss of memory lasting from a few minutes to several hours.

Between the attacks of all forms of epilepsy the patient is perfectly normal. He can work and sometimes exhibits exceptional brilliance. Napoleon, Mohammed, Peter the Great, and Julius Caesar (certain victims of epilepsy) are examples of those with well-developed mental faculties.   H.K.S.

SEE ALSO: CONVULSION, ELECTROENCEPHALOGRAPH

Epinephrine see Adrenalin

Epiphyte (EPP-uh-fyte) An epiphyte is a PLANT which grows attached to another plant. It derives no food from its host, only support and better light conditions. Its roots take water and minerals from the air, and the decayed matter found on its host plant.

SEE: ORCHID, PARASITE

Many orchids and members of the pineapple family, including Spanish moss, are epiphytes

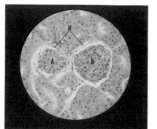

In this section of a kidney filter sac, the areas (A) are clusters of fine blood vessels. The thin protective covering (B) is called simple squamous epithelium.

Photo-micrograph by National Teaching Aids, Inc.

Epithelial tissue (epp-uh-THEE-lee-uhl) Epithelium is one of the four basic kinds of tissue. The other three are muscle, nervous, and connective tissues. Epithelial tissue either covers the outside of a body wall or lines a cavity. Its inner surface rests upon a basement membrane. Epithelial cells are cemented together by an intercellular substance and occur in sheets. Materials diffuse to and from these cells from underlying capillaries.

There are only three kinds of cells making up epithelium. These are classified according to shape. Flat ones that are wider than they are long are *squamous* cells. *Columnar* cells are taller than they are wide. In *cuboidal* cells, height and length are about equal. If an epithelium is composed of one sheet of cells it is called simple *epithelium*. *Stratified epithelium* is formed from more than one sheet of cells. Only the outer cells of layered epithelium are typically shaped.

Cilia may occur on free surfaces of any epithelium except squamous. Small intestinal columnar cells bear fine extensions, microvilli. Glandular epithelia may have one- or many-celled glands. Multicellular glands have tubular or flask-shaped secretory units.

J. C. K.

SEE ALSO: GLANDULAR TISSUE, HISTOLOGY

Epoch (EPP-uhk) In geology, an epoch is a subdivision, or part, of a geologic period of time. The period is, in turn, part of a geologic era. For example, the CENOZOIC ERA is divided into two periods. The first of these, the Quaternary period, is divided into two epochs—Pleistocene and Recent.

SEE: GEOLOGIC TIME TABLE

Equation An equation in MATHEMATICS asks a question or makes an assertion. An equation can usually be identified by the presence of an equal sign ($=$). The equation $x + 2 = 6$ asks: "Is there a number such that when 2 is added to it, the sum will be 6?" The answer is: "Yes. The number 4."

The equation $x + 3 = x$ asks: "Is there a number such that when 3 is added to it the number remains unchanged?" The answer is: "No. There is no such number."

An equation which asks a question is called a *conditional equation*.

An equation of the form
$$X + 1 = 1 + X$$
does not ask a question. It asserts that for any number X, $X + 1 = 1 + X$. This type of an equation is called an *identity*.

I. K. F.

SEE ALSO: ALGEBRA, ARITHMETIC

Equator (ih-KWAY-ter) The equator is an imaginary circle around the middle of the EARTH. It is equally distant from both the North and South Poles. It is the dividing line between the Northern Hemisphere and the Southern Hemisphere.

In ASTRONOMY, the celestial equator is an imaginary circle in the sky formed where the celestial sphere would be crossed by a line drawn up from Earth's equator.

The equator divides Earth into two parts

Courtesy Society For Visual Education, Inc.

✳ **THINGS TO DO**

ESTABLISHING PHYSICAL EQUILIBRIUM

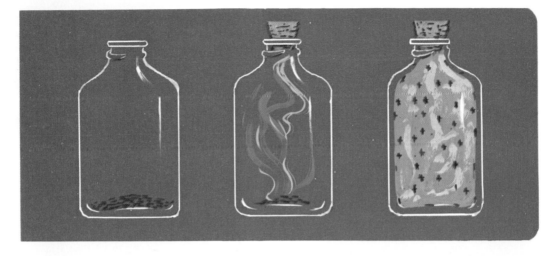

1   Place some iodine crystals in a bottle. Stopper the bottle.
2   After a short period, some of the iodine evaporates and the bottle fills with a purple gas. Later, the color of the gas no longer changes.
3   What has happened is that a particle of iodine, an iodine molecule, has escaped to the gas phase, and one of the gaseous molecules has collided with the solid material and stuck. Even though there is a change, one can not observe this change. When the number of molecules escaping the surface equals the number of molecules striking the surface and sticking, equilibrium is established.

                                                    J.R.S.

Equilibrium (ee-kwuh-LIBB-ree-um) Most chemical reactions do not proceed very rapidly, nor do they reach completion. When two reactions occur in such a way that their rates are equal but their effects are opposite, it may seem that the reaction has stopped. When this happens, a state of equilibrium has been reached.

Physical equilibrium can be similarly defined. Two or more forces may act on an object in such a way that the forces balance each other and leave the object unmoved. A state of equilibrium then exists.

If a rubber ball is dropped into a pond of water, it floats. A state of equilibrium exists. The forces pushing downward on the ball are equal to the forces pushing upward.

Equilibrium in living organisms refers to the state of balance maintained by living things in relation to the earth's GRAVITY. All animals have a center of gravity. This center in animals with appendages may be some distance from, or well above, the base of the animals. The earthworm has little trouble keeping its equilibrium, while the giraffe needs several sensory receptors to help it keep its body position in relation to its environment.

In vertebrates the sense receptors are the eyes, the semicircular canals in the labyrinth of the ears, muscle spindles, and the sympathetic nerve endings in the abdominal organs. All these receptors send messages to the brain to indicate the position of the body in relation to the center of the earth.

                                                    J. R. S.

SEE ALSO: BUOYANCY, EAR, HOMEOSTASIS

Equilibrium of forces see Forces

On about March 21 and September 21, neither pole tilts toward the sun. These days are called *equinoxes*

On about December 21 (winter solstice), the North Pole slants farthest away from the sun and receives minimum heat

All pictures courtesy Society For Visual Education, Inc.
On about June 21 (summer solstice), the North Pole slants most toward the sun and receives maximum heat

Equinox During the winter season there are more hours of darkness than of light in each 24 hours. During the summer there are more hours of light than of darkness in each 24 hours. Twice each year there are days with equal hours of light and darkness. These days of equal light and dark occur at the time of year called the equinox. The word *equinox* means "equal night."

One equinox occurs about March 21. This is called the spring or *vernal equinox*. The other equinox occurs about September 21

and is called the *autumnal equinox*. In the Northern Hemisphere the period from the vernal to the autumnal equinox contains the SEASONS spring and summer. From the autumnal to the vernal equinox are autumn and winter in the Northern Hemisphere.

The earth's axis is inclined 23½ degrees from a perpendicular to the plane of its orbit. As the earth revolves around the sun in the course of a year, each position of the axis is parallel to every other position of the axis in the orbit. This is termed *parallelism*. The sun's vertical rays migrate north and south of the equator but are directly overhead at the equinoxes. J. D. B.
SEE ALSO: DAY AND NIGHT, EARTH

Era (IRR-uh) In geology, an era is a major division of geologic time. The five geologic eras are the ARCHEOZOIC ERA, the PROTEROZOIC ERA, the PALEOZOIC ERA, the MESOZOIC ERA, and the CENOZOIC ERA.
SEE: GEOLOGIC TIME TABLE

Erbium Erbium is one of the RARE-EARTH metallic elements. Carl G. Mosander discovered it in 1843. It appears in minerals often found in veins of granite or pegmatite. Erbium is dark gray in color.

Erbium (symbol Er) can be obtained by crystallization of its bromates, occurring when they are cooled below 2800° F. (1538° C.). Its commonest oxide is rose-red, formula Er_2O_3. Erbium also forms many other colored compounds. Metallic erbium has interesting anti-magnetic properties at low temperatures. Its atomic number is 68; its atomic weight is 167.26; and its specific gravity is 4.77. D.E.Z.
SEE ALSO: ATOM, ELEMENTS

Erg An erg (abbreviated e) is a unit of WORK or energy equal to the work done by a force of one DYNE when it causes the object to which the force is applied to move one centimeter in the direction of the applied force.
SEE: FORCES, MEASUREMENT

Ermine see Weasel

✳ THINGS TO DO

HOW CAN GRAIN FARMERS SAVE THEIR TOPSOIL?

Materials: 3 large aluminum foil cake pans, rubber tubing, clay, soil and sand mixture, topsoil, cereal grain, dishes

1 Cut a hole near the top rim on one side of each pan. Tape a piece of rubber tube to each hole.

2 Put layers of clay, soil, and sand mixture in each. Add a top layer of rich topsoil.

3 Rest one end of each pan on a block of wood to elevate it at a 30 degree angle. The hose on the opposite end should be directed into a dish to collect the water.

4 In one pan make rows across the width of the pan and plant a cereal grain—wheat, oats, or barley.

5 In the second pan make rows the length of the pan and plant the same cereal grain.

6 Do not plant anything in the third field.

7 With a sprinkling can pour the same amount of water (rain) over each pan.

8 What happens to the topsoil in each case? Measure the amount of soil that leaves the tube and settles in the collecting dishes.

9 The first field illustrates contour farming where the farmer sows the seeds around a hill. In the second field the rows go up and down the hill. This prevents more soil erosion than the third field but is not as efficient as the first method.

Erosion Erosion is the wearing down and carrying away of earth materials. This is done mainly by the action of running water and wind. When topsoil is eroded and carried away, many plants cannot live. In time the barren ground that is left will be cut by gullies and a dust bowl may develop.

WEATHERING is the breaking down of earth materials. Erosion is the transportation of the weathered material. Rock, as well as soil, may become eroded. When running water follows the same general path over a long period of time, a *gully* will be formed. If this continues over hundreds of years, a canyon will result. The Grand Canyon is a good ex-

ample of erosion and the force of running water.

Soil erosion is a major problem in the field of agriculture and forestry. Most farmers today are following good practices of soil management involving soil conservation. These include contour plowing, strip cropping, terrace construction, and the planting of cover crops such as grasses and legumes. They aid in controlling soil erosion. Gener-

Mesas and buttes (small mesas) are upland areas that have eroded

Courtesy Society For Visual Education, Inc.

All pictures courtesy Society For Visual Education, Inc.
The Grand Canyon was eroded by the Colorado River millions of years ago

ally, the steeper the land the greater the need of following soil conservation practices.

Coastal regions are being continually eroded by waves and tides. Seawalls help prevent this type of erosion.   H. S. G.

SEE ALSO: CONSERVATION OF NATURE, GEOLOGY, WEATHERING

Erythrocyte see Blood

Escarpment (ess-KARP-muhnt) Escarpment is a geological term describing a long line of steep cliffs made by faulting or EROSION. A *fault-scarp* is due to FAULTING. A *cuesta* is the name for an escarpment caused by erosion.

SEE: GEOLOGY, MOUNTAINS

A dramatic example of an escarpment
Courtesy Society For Visual Education, Inc.

Esker An esker is a long, narrow, winding ridge made of coarse sand and gravel. It forms from sediments deposited by streams that flow through tunnels within and beneath a melting glacier. It appears as a ridge only after the entire glacier has melted.

Eskers range in size from 2 to 200 meters (6.56 to 656.17 feet) high, in width up to 3 kilometers (1.86 miles), and in length from 100 meters (328.08 feet) to over 500 kilometers (310.69 miles). The longer eskers are often broken up into segments and have steep slopes. Most eskers are found in areas of low relief and tend to lie in the direction of flow from the last glacier.

Eskers usually form at a time when the glacial ice is stagnant and thin. Melted ice from the surface moves downward through fractures and CREVASSES and accumulates at the base of the glacier, where it forms tunnels and deposits sediment. When the glacier melts completely, only the layers of sediment remain. A good example of an esker can be seen east of Great Bear Lake, Northwest Territories, Canada.   P.P.S.

SEE ALSO: GLACIER

Esophagus see Digestive system

Essential oils Essential oils are the volatile, odorous, usually liquid substances found in certain plants which give odor and flavor to those plants. TURPENTINE is one example. Other essential oils give odor and flavor to consumer goods like PERFUME and chewing gum.

SEE: RESIN

Ester An ester is an organic chemical compound formed by the reaction between an acid and an ALCOHOL. In this reaction, the hydrogen of the acid is replaced by carbon from the alcohol, and a molecule of water is formed.

SEE: ACIDS AND BASES, FAT, ORGANIC COMPOUND, SOAP

Estivation (ess-tuh-VAY-shun) Estivation describes an almost completely quiet state which a plant or animal goes through to adapt itself to abnormally dry or hot living conditions. The organism withdraws to a cooler, wetter place, or its METABOLISM slows, or both.

SEE: HIBERNATION

Estrogen (ESS-truh-junn) Estrogens are a group of HORMONES that bring about the development of female characteristics. The rounded body shape, fine facial hair, higher-pitched voice, and well-developed breasts are examples of these female characteristics.

Several estrogens have been isolated from animal and plant tissues. Urine and tissues of the placenta, testes, and adrenal cortex also yield estrogens. Since estrogens, as well as male androgens, occur in both sexes, their effects probably depend on the balance between them. All estrogens are steroid compounds. The common ones are *estrone, estriol,* and *estradiol.* Estradiol is the most potent and is assumed to be the functionally active one. J. C. K.

SEE ALSO: ANDROGEN, ESTROUS CYCLE, MENSTRUATION, STEROID

Estrous cycle (ESS-truss) The estrous cycle is the period when a female mammal is in estrus or "heat." At this time, the female will receive a male. The last part of the cycle is marked by changes in the walls of the vagina and uterus. Cycles are under nervous and hormonal control. The hormones are secreted by the gonads (ovary and testes) and pituitary gland.

In higher primates (man, apes) the estrous cycle is replaced by bleeding periods called menstruation. These periods end the cycle and do not correspond to the time of ovulation (release of eggs from the ovary). Tissue is lost during menstruation. J.C.K.

SEE ALSO: MAMMALIA, MENSTRUATION, OVULATION, REPRODUCTIVE SYSTEM

Estuary (ESS-choo-air-ee) An estuary is a funnel-shaped BAY formed when the sea invades a river valley at the point where the RIVER empties. It happens only where the shoreline is sinking or depressed.

SEE: GEOLOGY

Ether Diethyl ether, known simply as *ether,* is the most important member of a whole series of ORGANIC COMPOUNDS called *ethers.* Ether is an ANESTHETIC or pain killer. When a person breathes ether he loses consciousness. It is no longer as widely used as formerly because it sometimes causes serious illnesses.

Ether is an excellent SOLVENT for many organic compounds. It is employed in industry and laboratories in this way.

Diethyl ether is prepared from ethyl ALCOHOL, grain alcohol, by mixing it with sulfuric acid. Since ether evaporates rapidly and the vapor forms an explosive mixture with air, ether must be kept away from fire. J. R. S.

Ethology (e-THOL-uh-gee) This is a rather new field of science. Ethology is a study of ANIMAL BEHAVIOR.

Ethology tries to clarify the reasons why animals perform complex patterns. Animals' actions may be classified as *instinctive, learned,* or a blend of these two theories. Ethology is a comparative study of zoology, evolution, physiology, and psychology. It concentrates on *innate* or inherited behavior—the ways of acting that are programmed by an animal's genes.

An ethologist usually does not explain behavior as the result of an intention or purpose that the animal had in mind. Some *stimulus* or releaser must cause an animal to behave in a certain manner. An ethologist traces patterns of behavior among related species. He or she studies the changes brought about by natural selection. Stress is placed on the activities more complex than simple reflex action. A duck oiling his feathers, a canary singing, and a hummingbird constructing a nest are fascinating behavioral patterns to an ethologist.   H.J.C.

ETHYL—PISTON RUNS SMOOTHLY

NON-ETHYL—"KNOCK" IN PISTON CHAMBER

Ethyl eliminates "knock" by preventing gasoline vapors from exploding at the wrong time

Ethyl "Ethyl gas" is the common name given to some automobile and aviation gasolines to which certain substances have been added. These substances are called *additives.* The additives allow the gasoline to be compressed more within the ENGINE than it would without them. This greater compression results in more power and better engine efficiency. It eliminates or reduces the kick back or "knock," experienced when the gasoline vapors are exploded too soon during the engine cycle.

In 1924, *tetraethyl lead,* $Pb(C_2H_5)_4$, came to be used as an additive in "anti-knock" gasolines. But since COMBUSTION of gasoline

containing only this additive produces lead deposits along the cylinders, other additives were put in. During combustion the lead is liberated into the atmosphere. This lead returns to the earth in rain and becomes part of the food chain. This has prompted the removal of lead from gasoline.

Ethyl is also a *radical,* or group (C_2H_5), obtained from ethane (C_2H_6) and is the basis for numerous ORGANIC COMPOUNDS. The ethyl group and HYDROXYL group $(-OH)$ comprise ethyl ALCOHOL (C_2H_5OH). Tetraethyl lead illustrates four ethyl radicals in one compound.   D.L.D.

Ethyl alcohol see Alcohol

Ethylene Ethylene is a colorless gas. It burns easily, giving a bright flame. Ethylene is used in the manufacture of plastic. The plastic, called polyethylene, is one of the most used plastics.

The formula of ethylene is C_2H_4. It is the first member of an organic chemical series, the *olefins,* all of which have the same general formula, C_nH_{2n}. All of these compounds possess two neighboring carbon atoms with a double bond (or two pairs of electrons) between them. They are said to be *unsaturated* carbon atoms—(as in the unsaturated fats).

Ethylene is made by the pressure-and-catalysis of "cracking" of the saturated gases, PROPANE or ethane. Some useful derived compounds that start with ethylene are: ethylene glycol (an ANTIFREEZE and artificial ripener of fruits), ethylene dibromide, and $C_2H_4Br_2$, used in antiknock (or "ETHYL") gasoline.   D.L.D.

SEE ALSO: ORGANIC COMPOUNDS

Ethylene glycol see Organic compounds

Eucalyptus (yoo-kuh-LIPP-tuhs) Next to the redwood, the eucalyptus is the tallest living thing. It can stand 300 feet (91.44 meters) in height. An evergreen tree of the myrtle family, it is sometimes called the GUM TREE.

The eucalyptus is native to Australia and is also grown in Florida and California. The broad leaves are bluish or green-gray. The

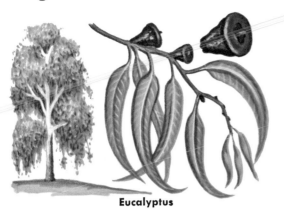

Eucalyptus

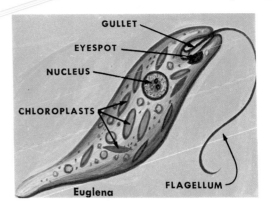

GULLET

EYESPOT

NUCLEUS

CHLOROPLASTS

FLAGELLUM

Euglena

rose or white flowers contain honey. The wood has a strong odor which insects avoid. It has a spreading root system.

Eucalyptus leaves are dried and an oil is extracted. It is used medicinally for nose and throat trouble and for treating fevers. The oil is almost colorless and has a pungent odor. H.J.C.

Eugenics see Biology; Galton, Sir Francis

Euglena (you-GLEE-nuh) Euglena belongs to a class of PROTOZOA (one-celled animals) that move by means of a lashing threadlike FLAGELLUM. Euglena is also classified among the simpler plants, ALGAE, because it has chlorophyll and makes its own food.

Euglena live in freshwater ponds among aquatic plants. They are microscopic spindle-shaped one-celled organisms. Covering the cell is a thick flexible *pellicle*. It is often striated or ridged. Inside, the protoplasm, or living substance, is divided into clear *ectoplasm* and granular central *endoplasm*. At the anterior end is a flask-shaped reservoir. Attached to the base of the flask, by a granule, is the flagellum. From the granule a small threadlike structure connects the flagellum to the nucleus. The nucleus, in the cell center, controls cell functioning and inheritance.

The reservoir opens outside through a pore. Opening into the reservoir is a large contractile vacuole. It prevents too much water from entering the cell and causing the euglena to burst. As water enters, small water vacuoles fuse with larger ones until the contractile vacuole is formed. This contracts occasionally, emptying excess water and probably some wastes into the reservoir.

A red eyespot occurs near the reservoir It is made of granules of a pigment called hematochrome. The pigment covers, like a shade, a light sensitive body near the base of the flagellum. The "shade" permits response to light from only one direction. This arrangement lets a euglena orient itself toward a source of light. Light is necessary for food-making (photosynthetic) activity.

Chlorophyll is contained in cellular bodies called plastids. The green chlorophyll traps light and furnishes its energy to the cell to make sugar. It is stored as starch in irregularly shaped masses. J.C.K.

SEE ALSO: ALGAE

Euonymus (yoo-AHN-ih-muss) This may be a vine, shrub, or small tree. It is the name for a whole group of flowering plants. The small FLOWERS are usually white or green. The fruit is often orange in color. The stem in most kinds is square.

The simple LEAVES are opposite each other. The stamens, petals, and sepals are multiples of or divisible by four or five. The pistil contains two to five carpels. The FRUITS of the euonymus genus vary. They may develop as a drupe, berry, capsule, or samara.

The wahoo, spindle tree, burning bush, and creeping strawberry bush all belong in this group. The climbing evergreen euonymus has aerial rootlets and can be trained to climb brick walls. They are all in the family Celastraceae. H.J.C.

Two kinds of euonymus

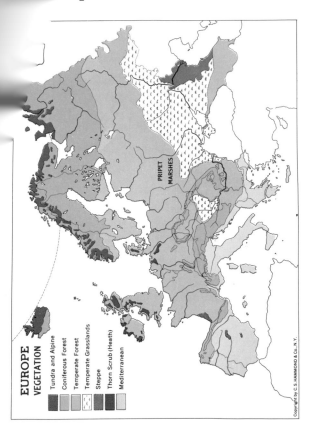

EUROPE
VEGETATION

Tundra and Alpine
Coniferous Forest
Temperate Forest
Temperate Grasslands
Steppe
Thorn Scrub (Heath)
Mediterranean

PRIPET MARSHES

Copyright by C. S. HAMMOND & Co., N. Y.

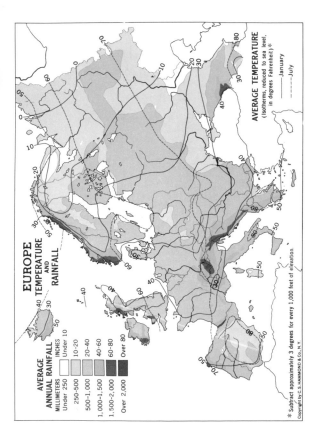

EUROPE
TEMPERATURE
AND
RAINFALL

AVERAGE TEMPERATURE
(Isotherms, reduced to sea level,
in degrees Fahrenheit) *
————January
- - - - - July

AVERAGE
ANNUAL RAINFALL

MILLIMETERS	INCHES
Under 250	Under 10
250-500	10-20
500-1,000	20-40
1,000-1,500	40-60
1,500-2,000	60-80
Over 2,000	Over 80

* Subtract approximately 3 degrees for every 1,000 feet of elevation.

Copyright by C. S. HAMMOND & Co., N. Y.

Europe Of the seven continents, Europe is next to the smallest. Only Australia is smaller. In spite of its size, it is the home of nearly one-fourth of the world's people.

LAND FORMATION

Europe and Asia are not separate landmasses like the other continents. Geographers often refer to these two continents as *Eurasia.* The Ural Mountains in Russia and Kazakhstan form the dividing line between Europe and Asia. The combined area of Europe and Asia is the largest landmass on earth.

On the south Europe is bounded by the Mediterranean Sea, on the west by the Atlantic Ocean, and on the north by the Arctic Ocean.

The continent of Europe covers 3,900,000 square miles (10,100,961 square kilometers), and has a total 25,000 miles (40,233.6 kilometers) of irregular coastline and many excellent harbors.

1. *Mountains:* A relief map shows that there are numerous mountainous areas on the continent. What the map will not show is that Europe has seen the successive formation of four separate mountain chains and the destruction of three of them. The most recent is also breaking down.

Ancient remains of the *Huronian system,* the first chain, may still be seen in northwestern Scotland and far-northern Norway. A second chain, called the *Caledonian system,* partially remains in north Wales, southern Scotland and central Scandinavia, where altitudes of 4,000 to 6,000 feet (1,219.2 to 1,828.8 meters) may be observed. The third chain, the *Hercynian range,* lies across southwest England, southern Belgium, and into central Germany. This arc may also be seen in central Spain and Portugal, in southern France and in some outcroppings as far as southern portions of the former Soviet Union.

The Alpine chain, which includes the Alps, Apennines, Dolomites, Carpathians, Balkans, Caucasus, and others, is the newest group of mountains. It has not worn down very much.

2. *Plains:* Much of northern Europe is made up of plains. They extend over northern France, the Netherlands, Germany,

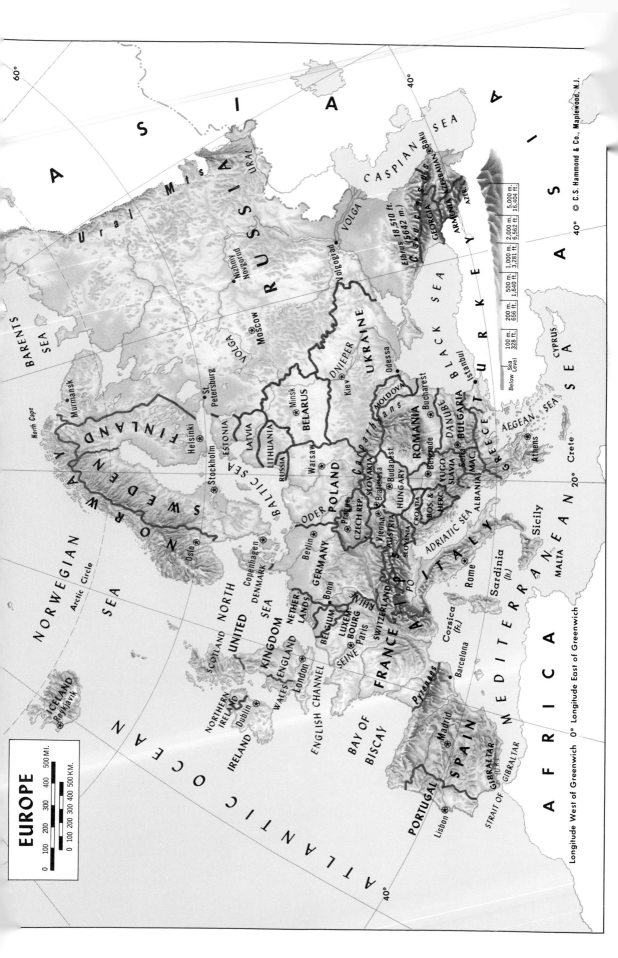

EUROPE

0 100 200 300 400 500 MI.

0 100 200 300 400 500 KM.

ASIA

A S I A

ASIA

RUSSIA

Ural Mts.

Ural

VOLGA

Nizhniy Novgorod

Moscow

St. Petersburg

VOLGA

BARENTS SEA

North Cape

Murmansk

NORWAY

NORWEGIAN SEA

Arctic Circle

ICELAND
Reykjavik

FINLAND

Helsinki

Stockholm

SWEDEN

Oslo

BALTIC SEA

ESTONIA

LATVIA

LITHUANIA

RUSSIA

Minsk

BELARUS

Warsaw

POLAND

ODER

Berlin

GERMANY

Bonn

DENMARK

Copenhagen

NORTH SEA

NETHER-LANDS

BELGIUM

LUXEM-BOURG

RHINE

SEINE

Paris

SWITZERLAND

FRANCE

ATLANTIC OCEAN

SCOTLAND

UNITED KINGDOM

NORTHERN IRELAND

IRELAND

Dublin

WALES

ENGLAND

London

ENGLISH CHANNEL

BAY OF BISCAY

Pyrenees

Barcelona

Madrid

SPAIN

PORTUGAL

Lisbon

GIBRALTAR (U.K.)

STRAIT OF GIBRALTAR

AFRICA

MEDITERRANEAN

Corsica (Fr.)

Sardinia (It.)

Rome

ITALY

PO

Sicily

MALTA

ADRIATIC SEA

SLOVENIA

CROATIA

Vienna

AUSTRIA

Budapest

HUNGARY

Bratislava

SLOVAKIA

Prague

CZECH REP.

Carpath

BOS. & HERC.

YUGO-SLAVIA

Belgrade

ALBANIA

MAC.

GREECE

Athens

Crete

AEGEAN SEA

DANUBE

BULGARIA

Sofia

ROMANIA

Bucharest

MOLDOVA

Balkans

BLACK SEA

Istanbul

TURKEY

CYPRUS

A S I A

UKRAINE

DNIEPER

Kiev

Odessa

Volgograd

CASPIAN SEA

Caucasus Mts.

Elbrus 18,510 ft. 5,642 m.

GEORGIA

ARMENIA

AZERBAIJAN

Baku

AZER.

Below Sea Level | Sea Level | 100 m. 328 ft. | 200 m. 656 ft. | 500 m. 1,640 ft. | 1,000 m. 3,281 ft. | 2,000 m. 6,562 ft. | 5,000 m. 16,404 ft.

© C.S. Hammond & Co., Maplewood, N.J.

Longitude West of Greenwich 0° Longitude East of Greenwich 20°

40° 60° 40°

Poland, Lithuania, Latvia, Belarus, and parts of Russia. The southern parts of Sweden and Finland are also covered by plains. This entire area was covered by the great ice sheets of the four GLACIAL AGES as were the plains of north central United States. This helps account for the similar topography, soils and to some extent, vegetation.

3. *Sea and land:* Throughout millions of years the continent has risen above and then sunk below the sea. During the time when the sea covered large areas, great deposits of chalk, coal and other MINERALS were laid down. The land is primarily the result of the formation and gradual breakdown of the earlier mountains.

The Black, Aegean, Adriatic, and Tyrrhenian seas were formed when the Alps upfolded. Elsewhere, large arms of the sea were completely isolated. As they slowly evaporated, huge deposits of salt remained. If Russia is excluded, no place on the continent is more than 500 miles (804.67) kilometers) from a sea or ocean.

CLIMATE

Europe experiences three main climatic types and several subtypes. The three main climatic zones are: (1) all of the west and portions of northwest Europe with mild temperatures and sufficient rainfall; (2) east-central Europe with more extremes of temperature and moderate precipitation; (3) southern Europe with mild to warm temperature and seasonal rainfall. A small area of extreme northern Europe has subarctic and tundra climates.

1. *West and northwest area:* Due to the presence of the Atlantic Ocean to the west, with its warm currents, and the prevailing westerlies, this part of Europe enjoys a mild climate with ample rainfall. London, England, as an example, is at a much higher latitude than Chicago, Illinois, yet its climate is much milder. The annual rainfall of this region ranges from well over 100 inches (254 centimeters) in western Scotland to under 40 inches (101.6 centimeters) in parts of the vast plains of central Europe.

2. *Central and eastern plains:* Land does not retain heat as long as water. Therefore, when the great plains of south Russia lose their heat in winter, they become severely cold. Since temperatures decrease with altitude, low temperatures prevail along the Alpine chain in a wedge that reaches as far

west as the highlands of central Spain.

In Russia, seasonal temperatures vary from a January average of 20°F. (−6.70°C.) to a July average of above 70° F. (56.7°C.). In winter the cold, high pressure areas push the warmer layers of air southwest and south. Under the summer sun the land quickly heats. The rising air creates low pressures, thus permitting the cooler, heavier air from the Atlantic to flow in along the same wedge-shaped route across the northern European plains. Rainfall is moderate throughout the central plains.

3. *Southern region:* Here is the famous climate of the Mediterranean portion of Europe. The Mediterranean Sea has a great modifying influence on this area. Temperatures are warm all year. The rainfall comes during the winter season. The air over the sea develops into low pressure and cold, moist air comes in from the north.

During the summer the air over the sea develops into high pressure. The area of northern Africa experiences low pressure. This circulates dry and relatively cool summer air over southern Europe.

RIVER AND DRAINAGE SYSTEMS

The formation of Europe is like a low mound, high in the center and low at the edges. For this reason, rivers of Europe flow from the center of the continent toward the seas in all directions.

The Seine, Rhine, Elbe, Oder, Vistula, and Dvina rivers empty northward into the English Channel and the North and Baltic seas. They drain the northern plains area. In the east, the Volga River of Russia and the Ural River of Kazakhstan and Russia flow southward. They empty into the Caspian Sea and drain the plains of Russia and Kazakhstan.

Other important rivers also empty directly into the Black Sea. One of these rivers is the Dnieper. Another, the Dniester, rises in the Carpathian Mountains and flows eastward. Much of southeast Europe is drained by the Danube. It rises in the Black Forest of Germany, passes through the Alpine chain east of the Austrian Alps, and flows between the Balkan Mountains and Transylvanian Alps across the plains of Hungary, Rumania and Bulgaria into the Black Sea.

On the southern edge of Europe, the Po drops from the Alps to the north Italian plain and then into the Adriatic Sea. In France, the Rhone River emerges from Lake Geneva,

NOT DRAWN TO SCALE

1 inch = 2.5 centimeters
1 foot = .3 meter

EUROPEAN WILD BOAR
4' long

JACKAL
2½' long

CHAMOIS
3½' long

IBEX
4' long

EUROPEAN
HARE
1½' long

EUROPEAN   ANIMALS

EUROPEAN ELK
6' high
plus antlers

BADGER
2' long

AUROCHS or
EUROPEAN BISON
10' long

WOLF 4' long

REINDEER
4½' high
plus antlers

OTTER
3' long,
including
tail

MOUFLON
4' long

FOX 3½' long,
including 16"
tail

WEASEL
1' long

RED DEER
4' high plus
antlers

CRESTED PORCUPINE
3' long with quills

STORK
3' high

SQUIRREL
10" plus tail

RAT 8" plus tail

SHREW
4" plus tail

BROWN
BEAR
6' long

MEADOW
MOUSE
3½" long

LEMMING
6" long

Some plants native to Europe

and passing between the French Alps and the Cévennes range, empties into the Mediterranean Sea.

A distinctive feature of European topography is the great system of undrained marshlands. The Pripet marshes in Belarus and the Ukraine have contributed to isolating western Europe from lands of the former Soviet Union. Most of these marshes are situated along the northern limits of the DECIDUOUS forests of the interior.

Similar marshes or bogs occur also in central Ireland and in Scotland. In the Arctic region extensive frozen marshes are found in northern Finland and the Kola Peninsula of northern Russia.

PLANTS AND ANIMALS

The wildlife of Europe is largely the result of ancient migrations from Asia and north Africa. Plant growth is determined by climate and the conditions of the soil. The distribution of animal life is influenced by weather and by location of plants and other animals.

Some of the animals which long ago roamed the continent have disappeared. Others have been mixed with domestic animals and still exist as crossbreeds.

1. *Animals:* The chief European carnivores (the meat-eaters) are the brown bear, fox, wolf, otter, and badger. Wildcats are still present, though they are not as numerous as they used to be.

European deer are still found in some numbers. Reindeer of Lapland are well known. The chamois, a member of the ANTELOPE family which lives in the rocky highlands, is found only in Europe. Muskrats are found chiefly in the French highlands, and moles are common throughout the region.

Rabbits have generally spread northward over the entire continent. The brown rat has almost replaced the older black variety. Domestic animals include large numbers of famous breeds of horses. Cattle, swine, and numerous varieties of sheep are widespread. Sheep are especially numerous in the British Isles.

2. *Plants:* Zones of vegetation roughly correspond to the climatic zones. Most forms are thought to have migrated from the east and southeast in prehistoric times when the land rose from the oceans.

a. *Mediterranean:* Spain, Italy and the Balkan Peninsula are characterized by many OLIVE trees. Plants in the region are of the tough, hairy leaf type well-suited to DROUGHT resistance. Woodlands contain evergreen oaks, Aleppo pines, and silver poplars. Smaller plants include oleander, myrtle, and laurel.

Higher on the cool mountain slopes are extensive growths of BEECH trees. Tapering away from the forests are bush plants such as heather, arbutus, pistachio, and the mint plants such as sage. Various forms of grass, including alfalfa, thrive in the drier areas, as do the bulb plants such as onions. CITRUS FRUITS were introduced long ago from the lands of the Asiatic monsoon winds.

No description of Europe would be complete without some reference to the hundreds of varieties of grapes which grow throughout the region. Grapes are especially well-adapted to the soil and climate of Europe from the Mediterranean region as far north as the southern end of the Scandinavian peninsula.

b. *Oceanic zone:* Forests of this region are typically beech accompanied by OAK. The region extends up into the slopes of the Alpine chain where cool, moist climate provides ideal growth conditions for beech.

Fruits are abundant in much of the area. Plums, apples, cherries and other tree fruits are plentiful. Grapes abound in this region also. Humid, dark brown soil is very important here for sugar beets and potatoes, as well as other root crops. Bushy plants include gorse, bracken and varieties of heath along the coastal areas.

c. *Cold forests:* Outward from the region just described, beeches disappear and oaks continue to appear accompanied by ash trees. These give way in the colder regions to PINE and birch which are extensive in the north and also the upper Alpine slopes. In this latter region, larch is widespread and typical. The soil of the pine forests is not suited to agriculture. Hence, there is little point in clearing forests for that purpose.

The pine and dwarf birch extend toward the extreme northern fringes of Norway, Finland and Russia where the TUNDRA is frozen most of the year. Vegetation is sparse, quick-growing, and the flowering variety. Moss is widespread throughout the region.

d. *Central plains:* The eastern regions of the Russian steppes and great plains show a marked decrease in beech and oak, which disappear somewhere near the Ural Mountains. In southern Russia trees appear only along streams and consist mainly of willow, alder and poplar. Herbaceous plants include the tougher GRASSES, HEMP, and the quick-growing varieties with underground food supplies.

Wheat is widely grown, along with barley, rye, potatoes, and some sugar beets. On the northern fringe of the region are pine, birch, and willow, along with grasses, heather, mosses, and lichens.

NATURAL RESOURCES

Europe is rich in natural resources, mainly coal, iron, and aluminum. Europe's extensive coal fields account for over half of the world's production. Most of these coals are of *Carboniferous* age. In Great Britain, the major coal-producing areas are Wales, the Midlands of England, and Scotland. Germany's deposits are mainly *bituminous* and *brown coal.* Major fields are around the Ruhr Valley and the Saar basin. In France and Belgium, the Valenciennes-Numur basin is an important source of coal. Russia has enormous reserves of good-grade coal in the Moscow and Donetz basins, and in the Urals, which extend into Kazakhstan.

PETROLEUM and NATURAL GAS were once rare in western Europe. Since the discoveries of large reserves of petroleum and natural gas in the North Sea, many northern European countries have become major producers. Russia's gas and oil resources have long been known, but only since the end of the World War II has Russia become a major producer. Smaller fields of petroleum and natural gas can be found in Romania, Germany, Poland, France, and other countries.

Great *sedimentary* deposits of iron ore underlie parts of Germany, France, Belgium, and Luxembourg. There are also rich deposits of *igneous* and *metamorphic* origin in Sweden, the Ukraine, and Russia. Minor iron ore deposits can also be found in Great Britain.

The greatest BAUXITE deposits in the world occur in southern Europe. These deposits generally parallel the Mediterranean, reach maximum development in France, and continue through many other countries. Even more extensive deposits of aluminum ore can be found in Russia. W.J.K./P.P.S.

SEE ALSO: COAL, CLIMATE, EARTH, NATURAL RESOURCES, PETROLEUM

✳ **THINGS TO DO**

WHAT FACTORS AFFECT THE RATE OF EVAPORATION?

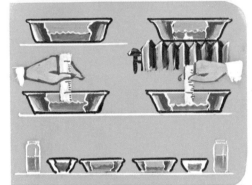

1   Pour a cup of water in a pan and set it to one side. Pour a cup of water in a second pan. Place this one over a source of heat for half an hour. Measure the amount of water left in both pans. What is the difference? The application of heat increases the rate of evaporation.

2   Pour a cup of liquid in each of three different sized containers—an olive jar, a bowl, and a cake pan. Let these stand for one day. Measure the amount of water left in each container. The greater the surface of liquid exposed, the greater the rate of evaporation.

Europium (yoo-ROH-pee-um) Europium is an extremely rare element. It was discovered in 1901 by Eugene Demarcay. He named it after Europe. Europium is included in the RARE-EARTH series. It is a metal.

Europium (symbol Eu) is elment number 63. It has an atomic weight of 151.96. The metallic salts made from europium are light pink. The metal is often found in deposits of phosphate gravel and sand.   J.R.S./A.J.H.
SEE ALSO: ATOM, ELEMENTS

Eustachian tube   see Ear

Eutrophication (YOU-trow-fuh-KAY-shun) This term refers to the aging of a body of water. It is a natural process of SUCCESSION which takes thousands of years. Man-made pollution is speeding up eutrophication.

Nutrients such as phosphorus, nitrogen, and carbon trigger a rapid growth of life. Fertilizers, detergents, and human wastes are loaded with these elements. When they get into lakes or rivers they cause an increase in plant reproduction. This creates *algal blooms.* A dense layer of surface plants cuts out the light from life under water. As organisms die the BIOMASS accumulates on the bottom. Decomposition uses up oxygen and increases the carbon dioxide level. Now the larger animals begin to die. This continues until conditions cannot be reversed and the body of water is "dead." Lake Erie is a good example of a lake going through eutrophication.   H.J.C.

Evaporation The change of a liquid, such as water, to gas is called evaporation or, in some cases, *vaporization.* After a rain one may notice that little pools of water on sidewalks disappear even though they could not run off. The water has evaporated into the air.

In order for a liquid to evaporate, the MOLECULES that make up the liquid must move faster and farther apart. This requires additional heat energy. As heat is absorbed from materials around the liquid, the molecules move faster and some start to escape from the surface of the liquid. Since the liquid absorbs heat from its surroundings, evaporation is a cooling process. H. S. G.

SEE ALSO: PHYSICAL STATES AND CHANGES, WATER CYCLE

Evergreen Evergreen means "having green leaves all year." PINE, FIR, and SPRUCE trees are evergreens. Evergreen plants are the opposite of *deciduous* plants which shed their LEAVES in the fall.

SEE: PLANT; PLANTS, CLASSIFICATION OF

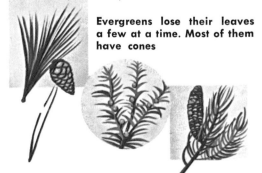

Evergreens lose their leaves a few at a time. Most of them have cones

CHARLES
DARWIN

GREGOR
MENDEL

JEAN BAPTISTE
LAMARCK

ALFRED R.
WALLACE

Many scientists contributed to the modern theory of evolution

Evolution Scientists believe that animals and plants of today have ancestors that lived millions of years ago. Instead of living in different parts of the world, these ancestors lived in the oceans. Of course, they looked very different from the plants and animals living in the ocean today. They looked more like the tiny cells which may be seen under a microscope.

A tree does not rise suddenly out of the ground. It grows slowly from a small seed in the earth. Each year it changes a little. After many years, it may have branches strong enough to hold a person. All living things change slowly. It took millions and millions of years for the ancestral forms in the ocean to become plants and animals living on land. There were millions of ancestors. Each ancestor changed a little.

Evolution really means *slow unfolding*. Scientists who study evolution study the ways in which plants and animals have changed. They do not always agree about the first ancestors.

EARLY THEORIES

The theory of evolution is the result of the combined efforts of many people. The ancient scholars tell the story of creation and the establishment of the natural order in the Old Testament. It is told allegorically. For example, the "day" mentioned is only a symbol of a period of time—not 24 hours as time is measured today. Species were created that were capable of reproducing themselves and the natural order was thus established. The growth, selection, and evolution which followed could have taken millions of years.

But many superstitions—such as that horsehairs in rainwater turn into living worms—had arisen among primitive people, and scientists began to study and develop what was finally called the *Theory of Evolution.* An Italian doctor, Francesco Redi, proved that flies came, not from dead animals, but from eggs laid in the dead flesh by other flies.

Evolution

Through the work of Redi, people began to understand that one living organism evolved, or came from, another living organism.

Several people began to wonder how individual differences arose among plants and animals. They wanted to know how new species developed. LAMARCK, a French scientist, decided that if a part of the body were used a great deal, it would grow larger with each generation. If a part were not used, it would grow smaller and disappear. Another scientist proved Lamarck to be wrong. By cutting off the tails of mice, he discovered that mice in each following generation were still always born with tails.

In the middle of the 19th century, two men, CHARLES DARWIN and Alfred Wallace, decided that the environment played an important part in causing differences to appear within the species. They pointed out that plants and animals depended not only upon one another for food but also upon a particular environment. As the environment changed, some plants and animals would die, and others, with characteristics more suitable to the new environment, would survive and reproduce.

A few years later, GREGOR MENDEL, an Austrian monk, decided that likenesses and differences between parent and offspring were passed on by means of factors, now called GENES. Genes are tiny units of DNA, able to copy themselves. When there is only one parent, the new organism is similar to the parent. However, the copy of offspring always differs slightly from the original. When there are two parents, each parent passes on a set of genes to the offspring. If some genes *mutate*, or change, likenesses and differences appear in the offspring.

NATURAL SELECTION

Plants and animals live in populations. They mate with members of the same species in the population and occasionally with members of the species in a neighboring population. For example, all cats in one town form a population of cats. Since they are members of the same species, they may mate and produce more cats.

Since each member of the population possesses a set of genes, there are billions of genes available in one population. These genes are distributed randomly throughout the population. Any member of a species therefore has access to many combinations of genes. However, once a mate is selected,

MESOHIPPUS
25-30 million
years ago

PARAHIPPUS
15-20 million
years ago

EOHIPPUS
55 million
years ago

PHENACODUS
70 million
years ago

PLIOHIPPUS
10-15 million
years ago

The evolution of the horse involved the change from a small animal with toes to a large one with hoofs. The changes were advantageous because of alterations in the land and food supply. The small wild horse of Russia looks most like the ancestral forms. Man has further helped the evolution of varieties of horses by breeding them for specific purposes

the genes available are limited to those possessed by the mate. If another mate were selected, another combination of genes would become available. Since some members of a species produce more offspring than others, their genes tend to become prevalent in the population. In general, those organisms that are best suited to live in their environment will produce more surviving offspring.

Every member of the population is free to select a mate of the same species and produce new combinations of genes. The action of the environment upon these new combinations is called *natural selection*. The organisms with gene combinations best adapted to the environment are most apt to survive and reproduce. This is what is meant by "survival of the fittest." In nature, many characteristics are selected again and again, while others are seldom selected. In the same way, certain cereals are always selected from the grocer's shelf, while others are rarely selected. Very soon, the cereals which are seldom selected disappear from the market. If cats with thin tails were seldom selected as mates by other members of the population, they would produce few offspring. The genes which produced the thin tails would become less prevalent.

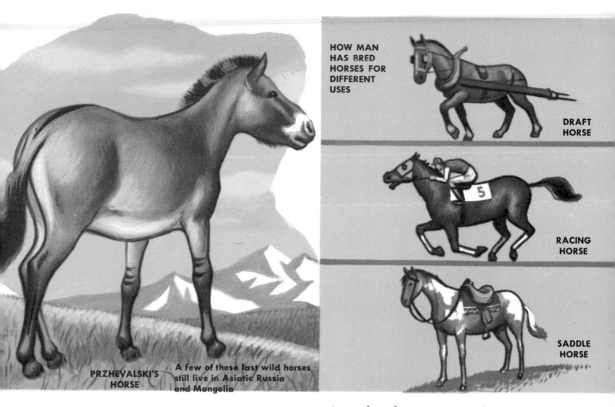

PRZHEVALSKI'S HORSE — A few of these last wild horses still live in Asiatic Russia and Mongolia

HOW MAN HAS BRED HORSES FOR DIFFERENT USES

DRAFT HORSE

RACING HORSE

SADDLE HORSE

ENVIRONMENTAL EFFECTS

The rate of evolution changes according to the environment. In the ocean, organisms have changed slowly. The salt and oxygen content and the temperature are more constant than on land. Some green ALGAE and the horseshoe crab have not changed for millions of years. On land, where major geological changes occur, organisms have had to change more rapidly. The building and recession of mountains and glaciers are major changes. In cold climates, animals have developed heavy coverings of fur or feathers, while trees have produced seeds that withstand the winter.

When environmental changes occur, organisms must become adapted, migrate, or become extinct. But living organisms must wait for genetic changes. These changes often come too slowly to allow individuals to adapt to a new environment. Organisms which are less specialized are more likely to survive. If, for example, the plants of a grassland were killed, the animals which ate only plants must migrate or die. Those animals which ate different types of food would be more likely to survive.

There are geographical barriers, such as islands, mountains, oceans and deserts. Organisms are cut off from one another by soil and vegetation factors, temperature differences, and distance. If members of one species moved to a new territory to obtain more food, they might live too far apart to breed with members of the first population. If the climates of the two environments changed greatly, the members of the two populations might develop new structures. Due to differences in breeding season, chemical make-up, or individual rejection, members of the two populations might eventually be unable to mate. Thus the possible exchange of genes would end and a new species would be produced. The time required to produce a new species would probably be at least a million years, since the changes are gradual.

By artificial means, man has created new species and subspecies. Man has isolated and domesticated many wild species of plants and animals. The dog, horse and cow have been changed in body structure and hair development. Certain viruses, bacteria, and parasites which are pests or killers of plants and animals have been changed to new organisms by chemical means.

649

THE PATTERN

As a young tree grows, it sends off new branches at the top. Smaller branches grow from these. The pattern of evolution is much like the form of a tree. One ancestor, like the first main branches, can give rise to many new descendants. The branches at the top represent the species living today. Often a branch, for some reason, dies. Other branches will fill the space or grow in its place. In evolution, as one organism becomes extinct, another organism, thousands or millions of years later, will fill its place.

Evolution is governed by natural selection and environmental change. Evolution can only change and remodel what is present in small, gradual steps.

FOSSIL RECORDS

Fossils reveal much about evolution, since they are the preserved remains of organisms. They may be skeletons, shells, or carbon prints left upon rocks. When an animal has been trapped or buried in ice, sand, or swamp, the entire remains are sometimes found preserved.

FOSSILS are found in different earth layers. Since high land piles over low land, the deepest layers are the oldest. Deep layers reappear when soil erodes or land buckles and rises out of the ground during earthquakes. The age of rock may be estimated very closely. An entire fossil layer is likely to be of the same general age as the rock layer.

Although scientists think that life began about 3 billion years ago, fossil records cover only the past 500 million years. Thus, many theories are proposed to account for the origin of life and the development of the first plants and animals. Scientists compare present-day organisms both with one another and with fossils of different periods.

THE COMMON ANCESTOR

Living creatures are composed of atoms and molecules. They are a direct product of the physical and chemical properties of the earth. As the gases of the earth cooled, billions of years ago, land, atmosphere, and oceans were formed. Living matter probably developed first in the OCEAN. Atoms combined to form molecules; molecules combined to form compounds. Eventually, ORGANIC COMPOUNDS, found only in living matter, were formed. As raw materials in the ocean became scarce, some molecules surrounded themselves with a thin shell of reserve food. They closely resembled the present-day virus, which is covered by a shell of protein. Finally, cells formed. They were probably surrounded by a thin membrane which kept the cell components separate from the ocean. They later developed a nucleus and were able to manufacture food, breathe, grow, and reproduce.

The great Irish elk developed larger and larger antlers that were an advantage in fighting. They became so large, however, that the weight of them was harmful and the species gradually died off

Chicago Natural History Museum

Early organisms began to find new ways of living. Some, like the virus, adopted a parasitic life, by living inside larger cells. Others started living on dead or decaying cells. Some cells developed molecules which allowed them to manufacture food by PHOTO-SYNTHESIS, like green plants of today. Many cells developed openings or mouths which allowed them to consume other organisms, like animals of today.

Most scientists accept the theory that plants and animals descended from a common ancestor. The most likely type of ancestor is the *flagellate*. Although these organisms form a technical phylum classed as plants, they are still considered to be both plant and animal. Like plants, they have chlorophyll and carry on photosynthesis. Like animals, they propel themselves with a whip-like flagella and trap particles of food, which they ingest.

THE FIRST PLANTS AND ANIMALS

The common ancestor must have produced at least three types of descendants. One type maintained the way of life of the parent and produced the modern flagellates. Another lost its plant characteristics and became an animal. The third line of descent lost its animal characteristics and became a plant.

The first plants were probably much like the one-celled green algae, which are successful in the ocean. Some algae developed different types of pigment, like those of the red and brown algae. This enabled them to live at greater depths where there is less light. Some became many-celled animals. For floating plants, a flat sheet of cells was an efficient type of structure.

The first animals were free to leave the surface of the ocean, since they no longer needed sunlight for the manufacture of food. They explored different types of locomotion, such as the *pseudopod* and *cilia*. Some, like the PROTOZOA, grew in size and became

Evolution of animals, like that of plants, probably began with a single-celled flagellate. Gradual development of two or three cell layers allowed more complex modifications

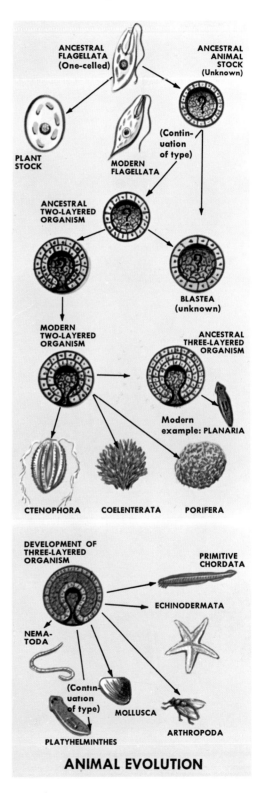

ANIMAL EVOLUTION

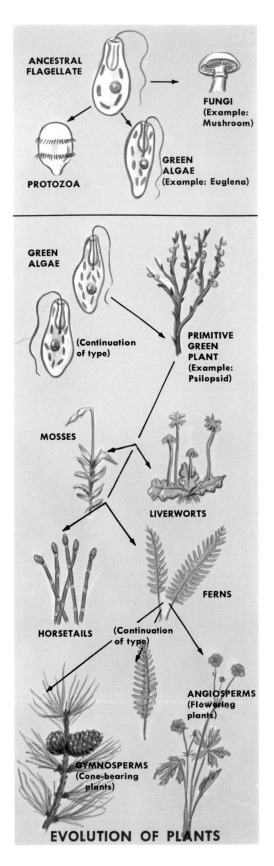

ANCESTRAL FLAGELLATE

FUNGI (Example: Mushroom)

PROTOZOA

GREEN ALGAE (Example: Euglena)

GREEN ALGAE

(Continuation of type)

PRIMITIVE GREEN PLANT (Example: Psilopsid)

MOSSES

LIVERWORTS

FERNS

HORSETAILS (Continuation of type)

ANGIOSPERMS (Flowering plants)

GYMNOSPERMS (Cone-bearing plants)

EVOLUTION OF PLANTS

successful one-celled animals. Others became multicellular. For moving animals, a hollow sphere of cells was a more efficient structure than a sheet of cells. The first multicellular animals were probably shaped like a hollow ball which consisted of one layer of cells.

The next step was the development of two and three body layers. Present-day animals like the sponges, coelenterates, and comb-jellies, are descendants of an ancestor which developed an inner layer of cells, called the *endoderm,* and an outer layer, called the *ectoderm.* The inner layer specialized in digestion, while the outer layer concentrated on protection. These two-layered animals, known as *diploblasts,* have remained in the ocean. The worms, mollusks, echinoderms, arthropods, and chordates are descended from an ancestor with three body layers, known as a *triploblast.* The third or middle layer, called the *mesoderm,* was an advantage. From the mesoderm arose systems for transportation for food and other body necessities. With this development the animal could increase in size, since food and gases could be circulated to the inner tissues.

GEOLOGICAL PERIODS

During major geological changes, such as mountain building, plants and animals underwent great changes. Scientists have prepared a timetable to represent these geological events. The first period is called the Precambrian Era. It is estimated that this time extends from 700 million back to 4 billion years ago. *Bacteria* and blue-green algae existed at this time. Fossil records for this era are incomplete.

Fossil records are more abundant for the three following periods. The PALEOZOIC ERA, which means "ancient life," began 700 million years ago. Every phylum of plants and animals in existence today was present at the beginning of this period. With the possible exception of bacteria, the land was free of organisms. At first, invertebrate animals and algae populated the ocean. Vertebrates appeared a little later. The agnatha or jawless fish, from which the present day LAMPREY EEL and hagfish de-

EMBRYONIC PARALLELISM IN VERTEBRATES

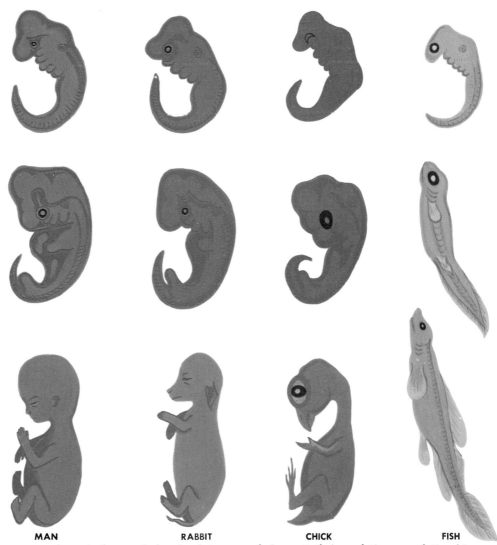

MAN   **RABBIT**   **CHICK**   **FISH**

Similarities among embryonic forms of the chordates reveal, in part, their evolutionary relationship

scended, were the first vertebrate fossils.

Plants were probably the first to invade land. The green algae produced tracheophytes, which developed roots, stems, leaves, and tissue, and reproduced by means of spores. Club mosses, horsetail, and ferns developed later, as separate descendants. FERNS grew to such enormous sizes that they formed great forests. One branch of lower plants became the bryophytes, or MOSSES. Gymnosperms, woody plants, began to replace the ferns. The conifers (cone-bearing members) arose then.

In the ocean, new types of fish developed. Fish with jaws replaced the jawless fish. Cartilage fish like sharks, skates, and rays appeared. There were three kinds of bony fish—the ancestor of the fresh water fish, the lung fish, and the lobe-finned fish. As the sharks dominated the ocean, the bony fish probably moved and later became the ancestor of the amphibian.

As animals moved slowly to land, spiders, scorpions, snails, and insects appeared. From amphibians, the first reptiles descended. These large, awkward animals were the first completely land vertebrates.

The MESOZOIC ERA, which means "middle life period," began about 230 million years ago. It is called the "age of the reptiles," since these animals dominated the air and water for 30 million years. They were ancestors of the birds, mammals, and modern reptiles (snakes and turtles). The largest reptiles were the DINOSAURS, which walked on land, and the long-necked plesiosaur, which swam in the ocean. Therapsids, ancestors to the mammals, were descended from the reptiles. These animals walked on four feet, developed hair and became more mammal-like.

Among plants the angiosperms or flowering plants arose from the cone-bearing ancestors. These became the dominant land plants.

At the end of the Mesozoic Era, many of the reptiles became extinct. The CENOZOIC ERA, which means "new life period" and which has existed for the last 65 million years, has seen the development of the bird and mammals. These animals have filled the places left vacant by the reptiles.   E. P. L.
SEE ALSO: ANIMALS, CLASSIFICATION OF; EVOLUTION OF MAN; GEOLOGIC TIME TABLE; PALEONTOLOGY; PLANTS, CLASSIFICATION OF

Evolution of man All of the physical characteristics of man show that he is an animal. He has gone through many stages of growth and development, as other animals have done. Human beings belong to an animal group called primates, which includes apes and monkeys. The animals most like man are the *anthropoid* apes. However, apes do not have the ability that humans have to think, reason, believe and choose a course of action at will. These abilities are what separates humans from all other forms of life.

Modern science states that man as a physical creature, and as he is known today, has gone through the entire evolutionary process to make him a separate species of animal. The evolutionary theory of CHARLES DARWIN gives the best explanation of how man as we know him developed. By looking at the entire classification—or taxonomy—of modern man, the line of EVOLUTION behind him—millions and millions of years of it—can be seen.

Kingdom—Animal (all animals)
  Phylum—Chordata (animals with a notochord)
    Subphylum—Vertebrata (animals with a vertebral column replacing the notochord)
      Class—Mammalia (animals that suckle their young and have hair)
        Order—Primates (monkeys, apes and man)
          Family—Hominidae (all forms of man)
            Genus—Homo (man)
              Species—sapiens (modern man)

The history of man is shown in FOSSILS. The first discovery of fossil man was made in the early 19th century. Since that time, the story of man's development has been pieced together. Often only single bones have been found. Sometimes these bones have been enough for men who study the development of man—physical anthropologists—to tell what part of the body they came from.

One thing that helps anthropologists in dating fossils is the geological layer of the earth's surface in which they were found. Over a period of almost one million years, four separate GLACIERS covered much of the earth. During each interglacial period—the time between glacial periods—there was a warm climate which helped evolution. The glaciers did not stop development because the animals could move south to where the ice did not reach. The fossils of man are usually dated according to the glacial period or interglacial period during which they lived.

MODERN MAN
appears 40,000 years ago

NEANDERTHAL MAN
appears 75,000 years ago

HOMO SAPIENS
appears 250,000 years ago

HOMO ERECTUS
appears 750,000 years ago

AUSTRALOPITHECUS AFRICANUS
and
AUSTRALOPITHECUS ROBUSTUS
appear 4-5 million years ago

RAMAPITHECUS PUNJABICUS
appears 15 million years ago

The Australopithecines did not deliberately shape their tools. They used what they found, such as a handy rock, for tasks such as cracking bones to get at the marrow.

Almost all human evolution happened during the Pleistocene Era. Scientists believe this era lasted at least 1,750,000 years. The Recent Era started more than 10,000 years ago and is still going on.

Scientists who study early human remains are called paleoanthropologists. They study fossils of human ancestors and try to establish relationships among them and a time sequence for human development.

Paleoanthropologists can find out the age of fossils by studying the geological layers of the earth's surface in which the fossils are found. Today scientists using special tests can accurately estimate the age of rocks and, therefore, the age of fossils, because a fossil is most likely the same age as the rock layer in which it is found. Fossils of humans are usually dated according to the glacial or interglacial period in which they lived.

It is thought that almost all human evolution took place during the 1 to 2 million years of the Pleistocene epoch in the Cenozoic era. The Cenozoic era is one of the time periods that scientists have mapped out on a GEOLOGIC TIME TABLE to represent geological and evolutionary events on the earth. Although the Pleistocene epoch included the glacial periods, these ice ages did not stop evolutionary development. This is because organisms could move to areas where the ice did not reach. Evolution also continued during the inter-glacial periods, when the ice retreated.

Fossil finds show that there were major physical changes during the evolution of humans, from apelike creatures to the modern form. These include increase in brain size; development of a chin; disappearance of heavy brow ridges of bone above the eyes; the change to a flat, vertical face; shortening of the jaws; and the shift to an upright (erect) posture. the increase in brain size suggests that humans were gradually becoming more intelligent. It was probably this, more than any other change, that helped humans survive the extremes of climate during the ice ages.

Paleoanthropologists have not yet been able to fit together all the pieces of the human-evolution puzzle. But they have identified from fossil remains major groups of prehuman and human ancestors that existed from 4 million to about 50,000 years ago.

According to most paleoanthropologists, human beings, chimpanzees, and gorillas all had one common ancestor millions of years ago. Scientists have been looking for fossils of such a creature. They once believed that fossils of an animal found in the 1930s, called *Ramapithecus*, was this common ancestor. They classified Ramapithecus, which lived from 8 to 14 million years ago, as a *hominid*, a member of the family that includes humans and humanlike ancestors. However, more complete fossils found in the 1970s led paleoanthropologists to conclude that Ramapithecus was an ape and was probably a direct ancestor of orangutans, not humans.

Most paleoanthropologists now believe that a creature called *Australopithecus* was the first humanlike ancestor. Fossils found in Africa indicate that *Australopithecus* lived there from 4 million to 1 million years ago. The first Australopithecus fossil was found in South Africa in 1925 by the Australian paleoanthropologist Raymond Dart. It was the skull of a six-year-old, which became known as the Taung Child. Since then scientists have discovered many Australopithecine fossils. In 1959, the British paleoanthropologist Mary Leakey found a fossil skull of a creature that lived 1.7 million years ago. She and her husband, Louis S. B. Leakey, named it *Zinjanthropus*. Stone tools found near the fossil remains suggested that this humanlike creature butchered animals. But wear patterns on its teeth indicated it ate mainly plants. Based on later findings, Zinjanthropus was reclassified as an Australopithecine and renamed *Australopithecus boisei*.

The most complete Australopithecine skeleton was found in 1974 by the American paleoanthropologist Donald Johnson. He called it Lucy, and dated the bones at 3 million years old. Many paleoanthropologists believe the fossils found to date represent four species of Australopithecines: *A. afarensis* (Lucy); *A. africanus; A. boisei (Zinjanthropus);* and *A. robustus.* The paleoanthropologists conclude that all of these creatures walked upright and had a brain about one-third the size of the modern human brain.

Many paleoanthropologists now think that *Homo habilis,* the first true humanlike ancestor, evolved from a species of *Australopithecus.* The first *Homo habilis* fossils were found at the Olduvai Gorge in Tanzania by Mary Leakey in 1960. The oldest *Homo habilis* fossil was dated at 2 million years old. It was found in Kenya by Richard Leakey, the son of Mary and Louis. *Homo habilis* probably made and used crude stone tools. They had a brain about half the size of the modern human brain. *Homo habilis* may have evolved into a more advanced prehuman form called *Homo erectus.*

Homo erectus, whose name means "upright human being," walked in an upright position, made stone axes and other tools, and probably discovered the use of fire. *Homo erectus* had a low, sloping forehead, with heavy brow ridges and huge teeth and jaws. They lived throughout the warmer parts of Europe, Asia, and Africa. The oldest *Homo erectus* fossils date from about 1.5 million years ago. Some of

The Java men were probably the first animals to cook their meat with fire. The climate of Java was probably colder than it is today

Early *Homo sapiens* used the bola—stones on the end of a leather thong—as a weapon. Accurate throwing made the thongs wrap themselves around the legs of animals.

the most famous *Homo erectus* fossils include *Peking man, Java man,* and *Heidelberg man.*

The bones of *Peking* man were found in northern China in the late 1920s. Peking man lived between 500,000 and 300,000 years ago, during the Pleistocene epoch. The skeletal remains of Peking man were found with stone tools and splintered and burned animal bones, which indicated that these people knew the use of fire.

Peking man made sharp tools from flint—a kind of stone. Hammers, scrapers, and simple instruments of bone have also been found. He ate meat, bone marrow, plants, and berries. Some people think that he may have had some kind of simple language.

Almost complete skeletons from several individuals of Peking man have been found, mostly in China. The adult was about 5 feet (152 centimeters) tall. He had no chin and still had the heavy brow ridges of the ape. His mouth and teeth were smaller than Java man's. Java and Peking man were closely related in many ways.

Fossils of *Java man* were found on the island of Java. The culture of Java man was probably similar to that of the Peking man, although no real artifacts—man-made articles—have been found that can be traced to Java man.

Heidelberg man is the name given to a form of *Homo erectus* that is represented only by a single jawbone found near Heidelberg, Germany. Scientists think that Heidelberg man lived about 400,000 years ago.

The first true humans, *Homo sapiens* ("wise human"), appeared about 250,000 years ago. Early forms of *Homo sapiens* had many features in common with *Homo erectus,* such as big teeth, heavy brow ridges, and a low forehead. But they had a brain that was equal in size to that of modern humans.

The best-known early *Homo sapiens* are the Neanderthal people. They lived in Africa, Asia, and Europe during the third interglacial period, from 100,000 to 35,000 years ago. They became extinct, or disappeared, toward the middle of the fourth glacial period. The first of many skeletons found was discovered in the Neander Valley of Germany. These people were long thought to be brutish "apemen," but paleoanthropologists now believe that the Neanderthals had a fairly complex culture that included a language, organized hunting for food, and burial of the dead. Families lived in caves or rock shelters. Their tools were made of flint and bone, and they were skilled enough to survive in the harsh climate of the glacial period. It is not known whether the Neanderthals were driven to extinction by more modern humans or were absorbed by the more advanced groups.

Neanderthal people had heavy brow ridges

and small chins. Their braincases, however, indicate brains as large as those of modern humans. They walked erect.

Fossils of another early *Homo sapiens*, *Swanscombe man*, were found near London, England. They date from about 275,000 years ago. These early *Homo sapiens* looked much like *Homo erectus*. Swanscombe man lived in forested country and hunted elephants, deer, and rhinoceroses.

Broken Hill man, an early *Homo sapiens* whose fossils were found in Zambia, Africa, may have lived about 130,000 years ago. Broken Hill man has features in common with Neanderthals and *Homo erectus*.

Homo sapiens sapiens, the subspecies to which all humans now living belong, appeared over 40,000 years ago. The Cro-Magnons are the best known of these early modern human beings. They are credited with the magnificent cave art found at several sites in Europe. They disappeared about eight thousand years ago.

Cro-Magnon people lived in caves. They were skillful hunters, killing mammoths, reindeer, musk oxen, horses, bears, and lions. Cro-Magnons resembled the humans of today but had somewhat larger skulls and more powerful bodies. Present-day humans are largely the same as the Cro-Magnons, with some physical refinements.

There are three main races of *homo sapiens sapiens*. Anthropologists do not know how they first became differentiated, although adaptation to varying environments may have played a role. The differences are not in color or nationality, but in such physical characteristics as head shape, bodily proportions, type of hair, ratio between head length and width (called *cephalic index*) and nose shape. The three main races are Negroid, Caucasoid, and Mongoloid.

Between 9000 and 8000 B.C., people learned how to farm and domesticate animals. Around 3500 B.C., they learned how to use metals. First bronze and then iron gradually replaced stone as the main material for tools and weapons. Also around 3500 B.C. writing was invented in the Middle East, and the historical period began, with people recording the events of their lives for future generations to read.

J.F.B.

SEE ALSO: ANIMALS, CLASSIFICATION OF; GLACIAL AGES; GEOLOGIC TIME TABLE; HUMAN BEING; LAMARCK, JEAN; PALEONTOLOGY; TAXONOMY

Ewe see Sheep

Neanderthal men wore animal skins as clothes. They probably dried the skins by pegging them out in the sun and used scrapers of flint for cleaning them

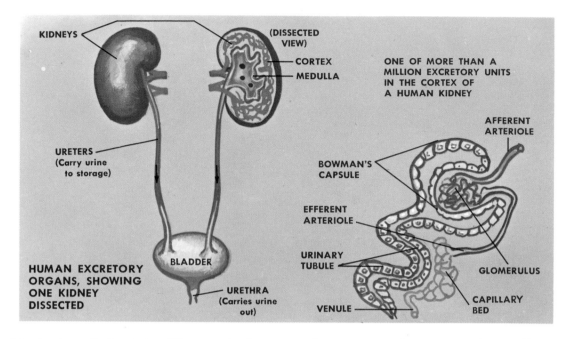

KIDNEYS

(DISSECTED VIEW)

CORTEX
MEDULLA

ONE OF MORE THAN A MILLION EXCRETORY UNITS IN THE CORTEX OF A HUMAN KIDNEY

AFFERENT ARTERIOLE

URETERS
(Carry urine to storage)

BOWMAN'S CAPSULE

EFFERENT ARTERIOLE

URINARY TUBULE

BLADDER

GLOMERULUS

HUMAN EXCRETORY ORGANS, SHOWING ONE KIDNEY DISSECTED

URETHRA
(Carries urine out)

VENULE

CAPILLARY BED

Exclusion Principle The exclusion principle states that no two electrons can have the same set of *quantum numbers*. The principle, stated by Wolfgang Pauli in 1925, is the basis of the periodic law. It gives the order for ELEMENTS fitting into the periodic table.

Four numbers are used to describe any electron. These numbers are called quantum numbers. The first quantum number is called the principle quantum number (symbol n). (n is any positive whole number value.) This number indicates the major energy level of electrons.

The second quantum number is the angular momentum quantum number (symbol l). (l has any value from 0 to $(n - 1)$ in intervals of one.) The angular momentum number indicates the shape of the atomic orbital. l numbers of 0, 1, 2, 3 indicate s, p, d, f orbitals respectively.

The third quantum number is the magnetic quantum number (symbol m). (m has any integer value from plus l to minus l. If l is 2, m has the following values, $+2, +1, 0, -1, -2$.)

The last quantum number is the spin quantum number (symbol s). (s has the values of $+\frac{1}{2}$ and $-\frac{1}{2}$.) The spin quantum number indicates the direction of the spin of the electron on its axis.

Quantum numbers are used to indicate the energy of electrons. If no two electrons can have the same set of quantum numbers, no two electrons can have the same energy.

A.J.H.

Excretory system (ECKS-kruh-tory) All animals must have a way to pass waste products out of their bodies. This is usually taken care of by an excretory system. In simple animals that have only one unit or cell for a body, waste is passed through the cell surfaces and also through the contractions of an organ-like bubble containing water and waste.

In the human excretory system there are two bean-shaped KIDNEYS, one on each side of the body. Each is connected to the bladder by a canal or duct, the *ureter*. The bladder, a sac-like organ, opens to the outside of the body through another duct, the *urethra*. The waste materials in the body are collected by the blood. As the blood flows through the kidneys, most of the waste materials and extra water are taken out. The mixture of water and waste taken from the blood by the kidneys is called URINE. It passes down the ureters to the bladder and is stored there. When the bladder becomes full, it is emptied through the urethra by passing the urine out of the body.

The basic unit of the kidney is called the *renal tubule,* and the kidney is made up of many of these units. The tubule begins with a tuft of capillaries, the *glomerulus,* surrounded by a capsule *(Bowman's capsule).* The glomerulus connects with a coiled looped tube *(convoluted tubule)* which in turn connects with a main collecting tubule. These tubules open into a part of the kidney called the *renal pelvis,* which is actually the upper part of the ureter.

The ureter, about 11-14 inches (27.94-35.56 centimeters) long, narrows as it leaves the kidney and becomes about half as small in diameter before it enters the bladder. The wall of the ureter has three coats or layers. The inner layer is of EPITHELIAL TISSUE with many mucous secreting cells. The middle layer is muscular, some of the muscles running lengthwise and some in a circular direction around the tube. The outer coat is fibrous and contains nerves and blood vessels.

The *bladder* is a hollow, muscular, thin-walled organ which is oval in shape when full of urine. When completely empty its walls are in contact with each other. The capacity of the adult bladder varies from 6-24 ounces (177.44-709.76 milliliters) of fluid. The layers making up the wall of the bladder are similar to those in the ureter. However, the muscle layer is thicker and beneath the epithelium is a submucosa tissue layer. This layer allows the freedom of movement between the epithelial and muscular layers necessary to an organ that changes size and shape. The *urethra* carries urine from the bladder to the outside.   J.C.K.

Exocrine glands see Endocrine glands

Exoskeleton An exoskeleton is a hard cover on the outside of an animal. It protects the soft inner parts of the body. The shells of clams, lobsters and oysters are exoskeletons. The opposite of an exoskeleton is an ENDOSKELETON (internal skeleton).
SEE: ANIMALS, CLASSIFICATION OF; CHITIN; CRAYFISH

Exothermic Exothermic refers to a chemical change in which HEAT is given off. Exothermic is the opposite of ENDOTHERMIC.

✳ **THINGS TO DO**

WILL GASES EXPAND?

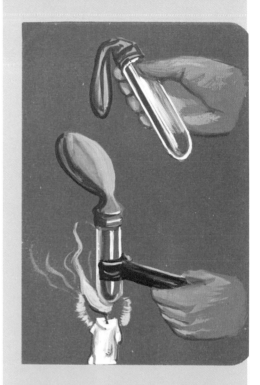

1 **Pull the mouth of a small balloon over the opening of an empty (though contains air) test tube. Using tweezers hold the test tube over a candle flame.**

2 **What happens to the balloon?**

3 **Heat makes the molecules of air move faster and farther from each other. Air in the tube expands. It escapes into the balloon causing it to fill up.**

Expansion Expansion is the increase in length, area or volume of a substance when it is heated. Expansion occurs in solids, liquids and gases. Gases expand more than liquids when the rise in temperature is the same, and liquids expand more than solids.

Substances vary in the amount of expansion for each degree rise in temperature. Among the metals, aluminum expands more than 2½ times as much as platinum with equal heat change. The expansion of mate-

✳ **THINGS TO DO**

WILL LIQUIDS EXPAND?

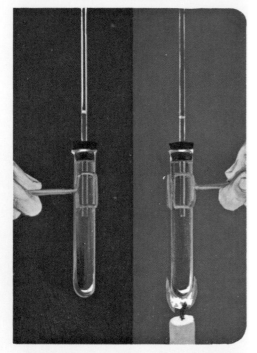

Materials: test tube, one-holed rubber stopper or drill a hole
in a cork, glass tube several inches long, candle,
colored water.
1 Fill the test tube with colored water.
Insert the stopper in which the glass
tube has been placed.
2 With tweezers or tongs, hold the test
tube over the candle flame.
3 Does the water rise in the tube?
Liquids expand when heated. Does
this explain the action of mercury
in a thermometer?

rials must be considered in all construction
work. The tar between sections of highway,
for example, allows the concrete to expand
in summer.

Water is an exception to the rule that
most substances expand when heated.
When water is heated from 0° C. to 4° C.
(32° F. to 39.2° F.), it contracts and
becomes more dense. Above 4° C., water
expands. This accounts for ponds freezing
on the top instead of the bottom, allowing
fish to survive under the ice.   J.H.D.

SEE ALSO: BOYLE'S LAW, GAS, KINETIC THEORY,
MOLECULAR THEORY

✳ **THINGS TO DO**

WILL SOLIDS EXPAND?

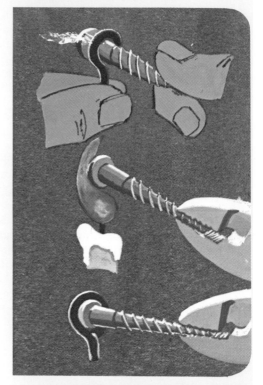

1 A commercial ball and ring may be
used for this experiment. A homemade device may be assembled with
a hook-eye and screw. The hook-eye
can be adjusted so the screw just slips
through the eye of the hook.
2 With tongs, hold the screw over the
flame of a candle for a few minutes.
3 Now try to insert it through the
opening in the hook-eye.
4 What happened to it? Metal expands
when heated.

Experiment An experiment is a test
made to confirm something which
is known or to find out something not
yet known. Taking the temperature of
boiling water is an experiment con-
firming something known—the temperature at which water boils. Exam-
ining the effects of a new chemical
compound on rats is an experiment to
discover what is not yet known.

SEE: SCIENTIFIC METHOD

Expiration Expiration, or exhalation, is the breathing out of air from the LUNGS. It is opposed to *inspiration*, or inhalation, the breathing in of air.

SEE: RESPIRATORY SYSTEM, TRANSPIRATION

Explosives Any substance which changes from a small volume to a large volume in a very short period of time and causes violent reactions is called an *explosive*. During the time it is changing from a small to a large volume, a large amount of ENERGY is released into the surrounding gases and causes rapid expansion, or the explosion.

Although explosives are generally considered as part of warfare, they have many peaceful uses. The blasts can be controlled and used to tunnel roads through mountains, dig canals, clear land, blast out rocks, and open mines.

A good explosive must meet several requirements. It must not explode under ordinary conditions. It must be easy to manufacture and safe to ship to other places. It must also produce the desired results. For example, GUNPOWDER must propel a projectile without shattering the gun barrel or injuring the person firing the gun. If an explosive is to shatter and lift stumps or rocks, it must do only this.

Most explosives contain the elements carbon, hydrogen, oxygen, and nitrogen, as well as other elements that help to determine the type of explosion which will result. Explosives may be divided into two or sometimes three groups. The cause of the explosion or the way in which the energy is released is the factor that decides in which group an explosive belongs. Propellants or low explosives, primary explosives or initiators, and high explosives are the three groups.

Propellants burn instead of actually exploding. They are often called *low explosives* as they are slower and less powerful than other explosives. Black powder or common gunpowder is a propellant. It is the oldest explosive and is used in firecrackers. It was used before there were guns. Smokeless powder, used in shotgun shells, is another propellant.

Primary explosives or *initiators* do not burn but explode from a spark, flame, or sudden jar or blow. They are used to *detonate* or set off high and more powerful explosives. They produce violent explosions with noise and shock waves. Mercury fulminate and lead azide are examples of primary explosives.

High explosives change from solids or liquids to gases very quickly. They are made to explode by the shock of another explosion. Guncotton, cotton treated with sulfuric and nitric acids, is a high explosive that explodes violently when compressed into a small space. DYNAMITE, nitroglycerine, TNT (trinitrotoluene), and RDX (cyclonite) are other common high explosives.

J. D. B.

SEE ALSO: BOMB, WEAPONS

Extension see Muscle system

Extinction (ex-TINK-sun) When the last plant or animal of any group dies, that species is extinct. Natural extinction occurs when one species gradually replaces another one. Several factors can cause a group of organisms to disappear from the earth: the climate, weather patterns, geological shifts, vegetation changes, or man. However, man is the only factor that can completely destroy a species in a relatively short time.

There has been a gradual succession of living things through geological history. There was the age of fishes; then the amphibians took over, and were overpowered by the reptiles, which finally gave ways to the mammals. When man arrived upon the scene this slow process of extinction rapidly increased. Ten thousand years ago, an average of three species disappeared per century. Now that average has jumped to fifty and is climbing.

During the Pleistocene Epoch early men were hunters who developed weapons they could throw. It was a period referred to as the "overkill." The giant beaver, giant buffalo, saber-toothed tiger, and ground sloth became extinct. The horse disappeared from North America but was later reintroduced.

People today kill animals for food, sport,

and fashion. As they cover the earth with selected domesticated plants and animals, they crowd wildlife into smaller habitats. Crowding reduces the reproductive rate and gradually forces extinction. Birds and mammals are hardest hit by human advances. We will never again see a moa, dodo, dire wolf, passenger pigeon, great auk, heath hen, Carolina parakeet, Black Hills bighorn sheep—large numbers of invertebrates and numerous beautiful prairie flowers.

Extinction can be avoided, or at least slowed, by greater public concern. We can improve wildlife management, set aside more reserves, save breeding grounds, enforce harsher hunting restrictions, use captive breeding, employ experimental embryology, and reduce the use of biocides.

H.J.C.

SEE ALSO: ENDANGERED SPECIES

Extrasensory perception Extrasensory means *outside* the senses. Extrasensory perception (called *ESP*) is being aware of, or knowing about outside events without any sensory stimulation coming from the events themselves. For example, if a child can describe a new dress her teacher is going to wear to school the next day, without having been told about the dress or ever having seen it, that child's knowledge may come from ESP. The outside event is the dress her teacher is going to wear. There is no sensory stimulation because her knowledge did not come from remembering what she heard (auditory stimulation) or saw (visual stimulation).

Many scientists believe that there is not enough evidence to prove the existence of ESP and that the methods used in obtaining the evidence are not accurate.　　J. C. K.

Extremities The extremities of an animal are the appendages. They may be more specifically defined as the extreme end of the appendages, such as the hands of the arm, the feet of the legs, or the pincers of a CRAYFISH.

SEE: SKELETON

Eye Sight is one of the most important senses of human beings, and the eye is the organ of sight. It is globular in shape. Humans have two eyes. They are located in two bony cavities in the front part of the skull which, together with the eyelids, protect them. The upper lids can close to cover and moisten the exposed portion of the eyes. This protects them from bright light and from foreign substances.

The inner portion of the eyelids are covered with a very thin membrane which begins at the top of the lid and continues over the exposed surface of the eyeball, extending itself as lining for the lower eyelid. This membrane, the *conjunctiva,* contains many nerves and serves as a protective covering. Whenever foreign substances, such as dust particles, enter the eye the conjunctiva becomes irritated and causes pain which continues until the substance is removed. The eyelashes also help to keep injurious particles from entering the eye.

The eyeball consists of three coats of tissues. Most of the outer coat is made up of tough FIBROUS TISSUE and is called the *sclerotic coat.* It is the white portion of the eye which can be seen. At the center of the eye, the sclerotic coat becomes transparent and is known as the *cornea.*

Behind the sclerotic coat is the *choroid coat,* composed of a vascular tissue which nourishes the eye. The choroid coat extends from behind the eyeball and joins with tissues called the *ciliary body.* It is chiefly composed of two parts, the ciliary muscle and ciliary processes. There are from 60 to 80 ciliary processes. They consist essentially of blood vessels and secrete nutrient fluids which nourish the cornea, the lens and part of the vitreous humor. At the front of the eyeball, in the center, the choroid coat becomes modified (changed) to form the *iris,* a ring of pigmented muscles which give the eye color. The iris has an opening in the center known as the *pupil.*

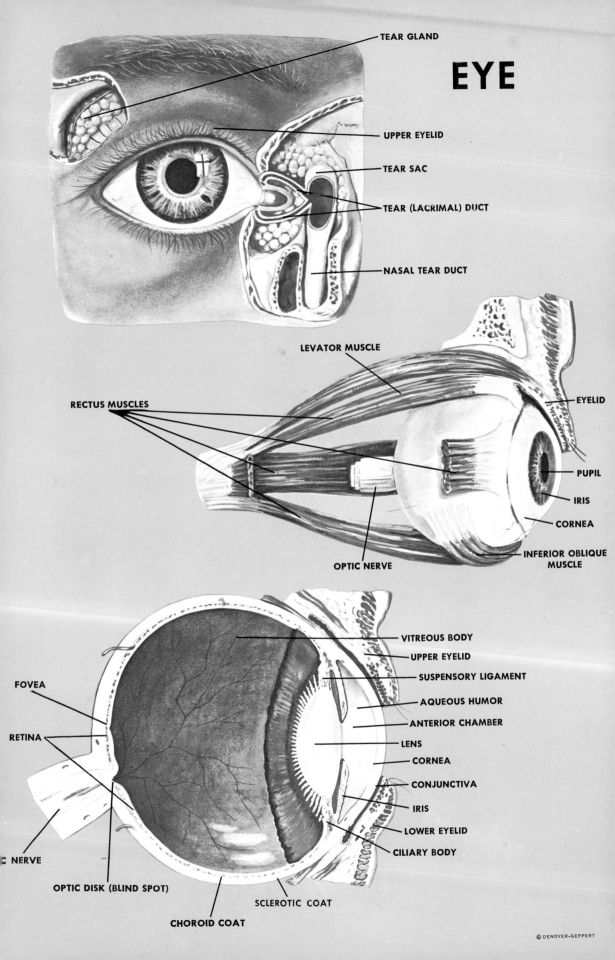

EYE

TEAR GLAND

UPPER EYELID

TEAR SAC

TEAR (LACRIMAL) DUCT

NASAL TEAR DUCT

LEVATOR MUSCLE

RECTUS MUSCLES

EYELID

PUPIL

IRIS

CORNEA

INFERIOR OBLIQUE
MUSCLE

OPTIC NERVE

VITREOUS BODY

UPPER EYELID

SUSPENSORY LIGAMENT

AQUEOUS HUMOR

ANTERIOR CHAMBER

LENS

CORNEA

CONJUNCTIVA

IRIS

LOWER EYELID

CILIARY BODY

FOVEA

RETINA

C NERVE

OPTIC DISK (BLIND SPOT)

SCLEROTIC COAT

CHOROID COAT

© DENOYER-GEPPERT

THINGS TO DO

WHERE IS THE BLIND SPOT IN YOUR EYE?

1 Put two small dark paper squares on a sheet of light-colored paper.
2 Hold this sheet at arm's length in front of your face. Close the right eye and stare at the right square. Bring the paper slowly toward your eyes.
3 At what point did the left square disappear? Did it reappear when the paper was moved closer?
4 The point on the retina where the optic nerve enters is called the blind spot since it lacks nerve endings. When the light rays from an object hit this spot, the impulse is not received.

ARE YOU RIGHT-EYED OR LEFT-EYED?

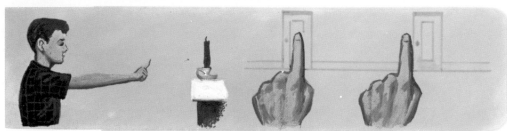

1 Hold your finger out in front of you. Line it up with some object across the room.
2 Close your left eye. Now open your left eye and close your right.

At which time did it appear that your finger jumped to the side? If the finger stays lined up with the object when your right eye is open, you are right-eyed.

HOW DOES THE IRIS IN YOUR EYES WORK?

1 Look into a mirror. Note the size of the pupils. They are the black circles —the opening in the iris, the colored part of your eyes. They are now adjusted to lamp or daylight.
2 Now have someone shine a flashlight into your face. Watch the size of the pupils.
3 Did the iris close down the opening? How does this help you see better?

The innermost coat of the eye is called the *retina*. It is the nerve tissue of the eye and is considered an expansion of the optic nerve. The point at which the optic nerve penetrates the eyeball is called the *blind spot*. Below and slightly to the side of the optic disc is a yellow circular area called the *macula*. There is a depression, the *fovea centralis,* in the center of this area. This is the point of most distinct vision. Behind the iris lies the *lens*—a semi-solid transparent body enclosed in a capsule. The lens is connected with the ciliary body by ligaments.

There is a space between the cornea and the lens which is filled with a watery liquid called *aqueous humor*. This liquid is secreted by the ciliary processes.

Behind the lens is a larger cavity filled with a gelatin-like material called *vitreous humor*. This material is enclosed in a capsule called the *hyaloid membrane*.

Above the eyeball is found the *lacrimal gland* or tear gland. It produces a fluid which keeps the eyeball moist.

To see images clearly, rays of light entering the eye must pass through the cornea, aqueous humor, and through the pupil, an opening which changes in size according to the amount of light entering it. The iris controls the changing of the pupil's size. The light rays continue on through the lens, which thickens or flattens out to allow the light rays to focus properly on the retina. The ciliary muscles act to change the shape of the lens. This power of adjustment of the lens is called *accommodation*. After passing through the lens, the light rays traverse the vitreous humor and finally focus on the retina in the normal eye. The retina is that sensitive inner coat of the eyeball which records the images. The impulse is sent along the optic nerve to the thalamus and the midbrain.

Fibers from the optic nerve make connections with cells in the retina. Because of their shapes, these cells are called *rods and cones*.

In the human eye, in the cell layer of the retina opposite the lens, there are about 125 million rods and seven million cones. These cells are the visual receptors for sight. The cones are concerned with vision of bright, colored light and the rods with dim, colorless vision. The rods and cones contain a photosensitive pigment known as *visual purple* appearing along their outer segments only.

The most accepted theories of vision explain sight as chemical changes in these photo-sensitive pigments that stimulate the rods and cones to transmit visual impulses along the optic nerves.

Movements of the eye are controlled by several muscles which make it possible to move the eye from side to side, up and down, and to rotate it slightly.   G. A. D.

SEE ALSO: ASTIGMATISM; CATARACT; COLOR BLINDNESS; EYE, BINOCULAR; EYE, COMPOUND; EYE, SIMPLE; FARSIGHTEDNESS; LENS, MAN-MADE; NEARSIGHTEDNESS; NERVOUS SYSTEM; OPTICAL INSTRUMENTS; OPTOMETRY

✳ THINGS TO DO

WHAT IS THE FUNCTION OF THE RODS AND CONES IN THE EYES?

1 Look straight ahead.
2 Have someone hold a sheet of colored paper at arm's length out to the side of your body. Can you see what color the paper is?
3 Slowly swing the arm forward until the paper is directly in front of the eyes. Can the color be recognized now?
4 The nerve endings called rods are located in the outer rim of the retina. They distinguish light and dark. The nerve endings situated in the center of the retina are the cones which are stimulated by color.

Eye, binocular Two eyes working together can see better than one eye working alone. In binocular vision (with two eyes) each eye registers a slightly different picture. Then the brain interprets, and combines them to give the single picture "seen." Such vision helps tell how far away things are. One EYE working alone is called *monocular* vision.

Vision with one eye is flat and dull (left); binocular vision gives color and depth (right)

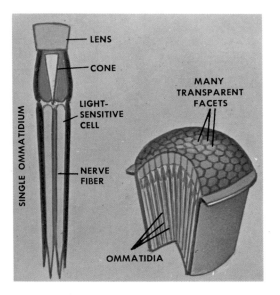

Compound eye of an insect showing facets

Eye, compound The compound eye (or *ommateum*) is made of many small eyes called *ommatidia* packed closely together. The common housefly has compound eyes.

The compound eye must be directed toward the light. When the light is directly over an ommatidium, the light ray passes through the transparent covering (*facet*) to the light-sensitive tissue at the opposite end. The light reaches and is directly over first one ommatidium then another, thus recording motion.

The sum of the resulting images sent to the brain appears either as a mosaic of dark and light or differently colored blocks. This visual process is especially well adapted for recording motion since any change in the position of an object affects the entire pattern of ommatidia. E. M. S.

Eye, simple The most simple "eyes" are single cells that respond to the presence or absence of light rays. These are scattered over the body surface and send impulses over nerves. In some animals like the COELENTERATA, these cells are gathered together to form a flat *retina*.

As soon as a retina forms, the animal may make a directional rather than a generalized response to light. If the retina becomes cup-shaped, light rays are more concentrated and the simple eye is more efficient. In some invertebrates, the cup elongates and becomes flask-shaped. This again increases efficiency by making a smaller aperture for the entrance of light rays. In many of the cup and flask-shaped eyes, there are lenses. Their presence allows for further concentration and focusing of light. J. C. K.

SEE ALSO: ARTHROPODA; EYE, COMPOUND

Advanced simple eye of a spider

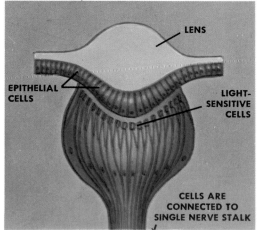

Jean Fabré

Fabré, Jean (FAH-bray, ZHAHN) (1823–1915) Jean Fabré was a French naturalist who devoted his entire life to the study of insects. The books he wrote are almost as readable as fairy tales.

Born in Saint-Leons in Aveyron, southern France, Fabré spent all of his life in that region. His poverty made it impossible for him to travel, so he studied the insects native to that small area. He was particularly interested in the spider, fly, bee, grasshopper, and wasp. Most of his knowledge was gained by direct observation.

Despite his poverty, Fabré managed to get a university degree, and became a teacher in the secondary school at Avignon. His textbooks in elementary science were used by thousands of children in France, but he was almost unknown outside of France. It was not until he was nearly eighty years old that people became aware of his greatness and rescued him from poverty. His most important work, *Souvenirs Entomologiques,* was recognized and honored by the French Academy, and the French government gave him a pension the last five years of his life.

D. H. J.

Factor see Algebra, Mathematics

Fahrenheit Fahrenheit was the name of a German scientist. His name is given to a scale used to measure temperature. The Fahrenheit scale has been replaced in most countries. The United States is the only major country using this temperature scale.

A mercury thermometer is marked at 32 degrees Fahrenheit (32°F) when the expanding mercury at that height is as cool as melting ice. The height is marked at 212 degrees when the mercury is as warm as boiling water. The space between is marked into 180 equal intervals, each a degree.

H. W. M.

SEE ALSO: CALORIE, THERMOMETER

Faint A faint is a sudden feeling of weakness, collapse, and loss of conciousness due to lack of oxygen in the brain. This results from an abrupt fall in BLOOD PRESSURE or a rapid change in body position.

Fairy ring see Mushroom

Falcon (FAWL-kuhn) Falcon is the name given to several kinds of long-winged birds. They are called BIRDS OF PREY because they swoop down from the sky, catching and killing small animals and birds. There are five living families of falcon-like birds, including the so-called "true" falcons and the HAWKS.

Falcons have strong, hooked bills. The edges of the bill are notched. They eat insects as well as small animals.

Falcons are found in all parts of the world. Species found in America are duck hawks, pigeon hawks, sparrow hawks and prairie falcons.

The American duck hawk is very swift. It can overtake almost any bird in flight and kill it by striking it to earth with its talons.

Falconry is a sport which dates back to ancient times. The females, usually of the Old World species, were trained to hunt and kill small animals.

I. H. S.

Peregrine falcon   James P. Rowan

Fall see Seasons

Falling bodies From the standpoint of common reason and observations made daily, it might seem as though a body which is light in weight would fall more slowly than one which is heavier. This was commonly considered to be the case until about 1590, when GALILEO performed his famous experiment from the Leaning Tower of Pisa. He demonstrated that objects of different weight, dropped from the same height, took the same amount of time to reach the ground.

Freely falling bodies are the most common example of motion with nearly constant acceleration. The acceleration of a falling body is due to the "pull" of gravity. This acceleration, *g,* is constant. The value of *g* at sea level is about 980 cm/sec^2 or 32 ft/sec^2. These values are accurate enough for ordinary problems even slightly above sea level. If an object is dropped from a certain height, the motion of the object is described by the following equations:

$$V=gt; H=\frac{1}{2}gt^2; V^2=2gh.$$

Here, V=velocity after a given time in free fall; t=time of fall in seconds; h=distance of fall. Note that the weight of the object does not appear in the equations.   A. E. L.
SEE ALSO: ACCELERATION, FRICTION, GRAVITY

Falling star see Meteor

Fallopian tubes see Estrous cycle, Menstruation, Reproductive systems

Fallout When a nuclear device, such as a hydrogen bomb, is exploded, soil, dust, and other debris are pulled up into the mushroom cloud of the explosion. This material becomes radioactive and, along with radioactive particles of the bomb itself, drifts back to the surface of the earth. This is known as "fallout." The amount of fallout depends on the size of the bomb.

Fallow (FAL-oh) Fallow describes land which is plowed and left unplanted for a season or more. This is done for the purpose of freeing fertilizing elements and admitting air into the soil.
SEE: CULTIVATION, NITROGEN CYCLE

Family see Animals, classification of; Plants, classification of

Fang see Snakes

Farad (FAHR-ahd) A farad (F) is a unit of electrical capacitance. One farad is one coulomb stored in a capacitor with a potential difference across its plates of one volt. The capacitance units are microfarad (MF), one millionth of a farad; and picofarad (pF), one millionth of a microfarad.

Michael Faraday and his induction coil

Faraday, Michael (1791–1867) Michael Faraday was an English physicist who discovered the laws of electromagnetism. Those laws, in addition to his discoveries of ELECTROLYSIS, are found in every physics textbook. His work in the field of ELECTRICITY made possible the electric light, the electric motor, and the DYNAMO. Without these devices, modern life could not exist.

When Michael was five years old, the Faraday family moved from Newington, Surrey, where Mr. Faraday was a blacksmith, to London. Life was painfully hard for the family, and Michael's share of bread given him from a relief line had to last him one week. "My education," he wrote, "was of the most ordinary description, consisting of little more than the rudiments of reading, writing, and arithmetic at a common day-school. My hours out of school were passed at home (the upper story of an old coach house) or on the streets." But Michael was ambitious. He found a job as errand boy for a bookseller and bookbinder. A year later he was made an apprentice.

He enjoyed his work primarily because it afforded him an opportunity to learn. The three books that introduced him to natural science and electricity were the *Encyclopaedia Britannica,* Watt's *Improvement of the Mind,* and Mrs. Marcet's *Conversations on Chemistry.*

With what money he could spare, Faraday bought materials for experiments, and by 1812 was investigating electrolytic DE-COMPOSITION. That spring a generous customer enabled him to attend four lectures by Sir Humphry Davy at the Royal Institution. He took careful notes, wrote them out in detail, and sent them to Davy with a request for employment at the Institution in any capacity connected with science. Davy suggested that he consider seriously before giving up the security of his trade for the insecurity of science, but when Faraday insisted, Davy hired him as a laboratory assistant. In March, 1813, he became Davy's assistant and accompanied him on a two-year tour of European universities. Many of the important men he met later became his friends and colleagues.

Upon his return to England and the Royal Institution, Faraday began research of his own, continuing as Davy's assistant. He experimented in the fields of electricity and chemistry, becoming an outstanding lecturer and earning honorary degrees and awards from all parts of the world. Faraday's services were eagerly sought by businesses everywhere for fabulous sums of money, but he preferred to remain in the field of scientific research. When he was sixty-seven years old, Queen Victoria provided him with a small pension and a house where he lived the last nine years of his life.   D. H. J.

SEE ALSO: DAVY, SIR HUMPHRY

Farm see Agriculture

In farsightedness, light rays are focused behind the retina of the eye. A lens corrects this

Farsightedness Farsightedness is a condition of faulty vision. The farsighted person can see a long distance, but nearer objects, or those within the usual range, are not so clear. About twenty people out of every hundred are farsighted. When the condition is severe or complicated by other EYE changes, it has to be corrected by glasses.

The basic cause of farsightedness is a variation in the structure of the eye itself, although this is not noticeable to others. The eyeball is not spherical but is shortened. This causes the light rays to come to a FOCUS behind the retina in the back part of the eye. It is stimulation of the cells of the retina which carry the "sight" message to the brain.

The new-born baby and the very young are inclined to farsightedness. This is not usually troublesome because the muscles encircling the lens can contract or relax, changing the shape of the lens slightly. When the lens becomes thicker, the light passing through it is focused more accurately on the retina, overcoming the tendency to have the focus fall behind the retina.

As one reaches middle life, the muscles and other eye structures, particularly the lens, become less elastic. When this happens, the eye loses its ability to accommodate itself to changing conditions, and the person is permanently farsighted.   H. K. S.

SEE ALSO: OPTOMETRY

IS FAT A GOOD CONDUCTOR OF HEAT?

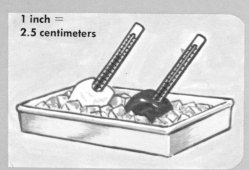

1 inch = 2.5 centimeters

1 **Purchase a two-inch cube of suet (fat) and a cube exactly the same size of lean meat. Leave them out of the refrigerator for at least half a day.**
2 **Check two thermometers for accuracy before beginning the experiment.**
3 **Insert one thermometer into the cube of fat so the metal tip reaches the center. Push the second thermometer into the cube of meat.**
4 **Set all of this into a refrigerator or pack in ice and check the temperature every ten minutes. Which tissue, the fat or muscle, gets colder faster?**
5 **After an hour bring both thermometers and cubes out at room temperature. Which one warms up faster?**
6 **Can you see why it is advantageous for a whale to have a thick layer of blubber (fat) under its skin?**

Fat Fat is a fuel food. It is found in cream, butter, the yolk of an egg, meat, gravy, salad dressing, and other foods.

Animals use fat as fuel, as they do CARBOHYDRATES. From these two basic foods—fats and carbohydrates—come the chief sources of energy. Fat yields twice as much energy or heat as carbohydrates. Carbohydrates can be changed into fat and stored.

Carbohydrates are used for quick energy. The body stores fat to be drawn upon when carbohydrates are no longer entering the system through the intestines.

The fat deposits under the skin act as insulation. Fat is a poor conductor of heat and aids in conserving body temperatures. Fat also protects to a degree against injury to deeper parts of the body.

Fats are the same as fixed oils. When an OIL is solid, it is called fat. Examples are lard, tallow (candles, soap), oleomargarine, and even some PLASTICS (which have esters in them).

Every fat has a MELTING POINT at which it will turn into oil. In the same way oil will solidify as it gets cool. Fats in body tissues are mostly the kind with melting points below body temperature.   B. J. C.

SEE ALSO: ESTER, TALLOW

Fat, adipose tissue (ADD-uh-pohs) Fat is a change in, or modification of, fibrous connective tissue. Some of the cells found among the fibers of CONNECTIVE TISSUE begin to store fat. In the beginning small drops of fat appear in the cytoplasm of these cells. As the drops of fat increase in size, they touch one another and unite (*coalesce*) to form larger and larger drops until the whole center of the cell is occupied by one large drop of fat. This is like the way two touching drops of water unite to form a larger drop. The usual parts of the cell are pushed out of the way and stretch out around the edges of the fat drop.

After many fat cells have been formed, the connective tissue seems less dense as its fibers are pushed aside to make room for them. Large numbers of fat cells become so closely packed together that they lose their round or spherical shape. A mass of them looks somewhat like a honeycomb.

An animal that is starving, or one that is hibernating, uses its fat tissue for a source of energy. When the stored fat has been used, the cells return to normal size and appearance.   J. C. K.

SEE ALSO: CELL, FAT, HIBERNATION, OBESITY

Fathometer see Depth sounding

FAULT IN EARTH'S CRUST

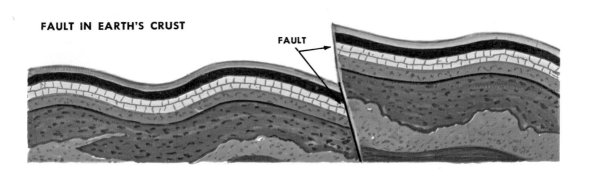

FAULT

Fatigue Fatigue is a feeling of tiredness and weakness caused by lack of sleep, extra work, illness, or lack of good food. Fatigue can also occur because of fear or hard mental work.

Muscle fatigue is a specific inability of a muscle to continue contracting due to over-exertion. The junction of nerves and muscles, where nerve impulses are relayed, tires very easily, and cannot transmit an impulse if there are metabolic waste products such as LACTIC ACID around. The muscles must be rested while the waste products are carried away, and then it can function again. Most fatigue can be cured by rest or sleep.   E.S.S.

Fatty acids Fatty acids are the main ingredients of fats, oils, and waxes. Before fats can be used as food inside the body, the fatty acids must be chemically separated, by digestion, from the glycerol to which they are joined. This same separation occurs when fats become rancid (sour). The odor of rancid fat is the odor of free fatty acids.

The most common fatty acids are *stearic acid,* contained in large amounts in animal fats, and *palmitic* and *oleic* acids, which are found in almost all fats. The saturated fatty acids, and hard animal fats, and processed (hydrogenated) fats are thought harmful to the body when taken in large amounts. They are believed to be a basic cause of hardening of the blood vessels (ARTERIOSCLEROSIS). Unsaturated fatty acids, such as the oils of fish and plants, are essential to the body and are much better food. Fatty acids are also used to make soaps, detergents, paints and resins.   J. K. L.

SEE ALSO: FAT, METABOLISM

Faulting A fault is a break or fracture in the earth's crust which causes the layers of earth or rock on one side of the break to be higher than those on the other side. Some MOUNTAINS are formed by faulting.

SEE: EARTHQUAKE, GEOLOGY

Fauna (FAW-nuh) Fauna is the animal population of a particular place or of a certain period of time. The term usually covers all animals of a given region during a geological period.

SEE: GEOGRAPHY, GEOLOGIC TIME TABLE, PALEONTOLOGY

Fawn see Deer family

Three types of feathers

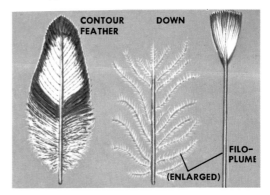

CONTOUR FEATHER   DOWN   FILO-PLUME   (ENLARGED)

Feather Feathers make up the covering of the body and wings of birds. Although feathers are small and light, they protect BIRDS from cold and rain.

Feathers are the outgrowth of the bird's skin. When a feather is fully grown, it is a nonliving structure.

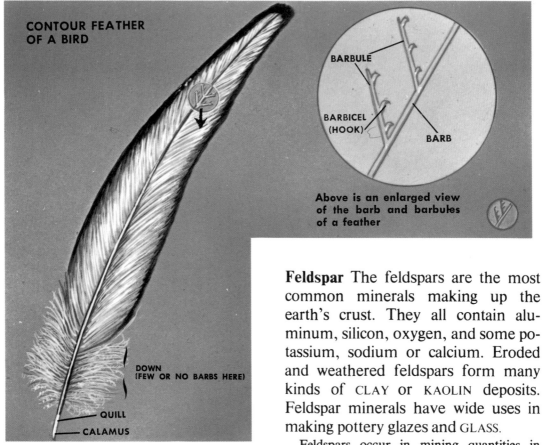

CONTOUR FEATHER
OF A BIRD

BARBULE

BARBICEL
(HOOK)

BARB

Above is an enlarged view
of the barb and barbules
of a feather

DOWN
(FEW OR NO BARBS HERE)

QUILL

CALAMUS

There are three main types of feathers. *Contour* feathers are large and include wing and tail feathers. *Down,* the softest kind of feathers, grows beneath the contour feathers. Ducks and geese have a padlike covering of down on their bodies. *Filoplumes* are hair-like feathers scattered over the skin between the other feathers.

Each feather has a center *spine* or *shaft.* Arranged along the shaft are small, parallel barbs from which grow *barbules.* The barbules are edged with tiny hooks, *barbicels,* which interlock with those of adjacent barbules, forming a mat-like surface. The barbs at the base have no hooks. The base of the feather is called a *quill.* The part attached to the skin is called a *calamus.*

The dull color of feathers is formed by a color pigment called *melanin.* Bright colors are formed by a substance called *lipochrome.* Iridescent colors are caused by the interference of light waves reflected through colorless filmlike layers of certain barbules. Color seen in soap bubbles and oil film is based on the same principle.   I. H. S.

SEE ALSO: SKIN MODIFICATIONS

Feldspar The feldspars are the most common minerals making up the earth's crust. They all contain aluminum, silicon, oxygen, and some potassium, sodium or calcium. Eroded and weathered feldspars form many kinds of CLAY or KAOLIN deposits. Feldspar minerals have wide uses in making pottery glazes and GLASS.

Feldspars occur in mining quantities in about one-sixth of the American states. The coarsely crystalline *pegmatite* rocks are good sources of industrial ceramic grades. Semiprecious varieties of feldspar include pale-blue *amazonstone* and *moonstone.*

Some feldspar crystals occur in lopsided box shapes

The two main types of feldspar are difficult to tell apart. The *orthoclases* contain potassium and the *alkali feldspars* or *plagioclases* contain varying amounts of sodium and calcium.   D. A. B.

Female see Heredity

Femur see Skeleton

Fen see Marsh

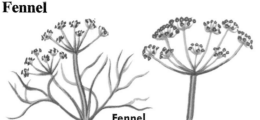

Fennel

Fennel (FENN-uhl) Fennel is a plant which belongs to the CARROT family. The seeds are used as a spice in cooking. Fennel grows in all parts of the world. It is a native of lands around the Mediterranean Sea.

The leaves are small and lacy. Fennel bears small yellow flowers. The fruits grow in clusters and hold tiny seeds.

In flavor, the fennel seed is sweet and resembles ANISE. It is used in Italian cookery and French cooks use it on bread and rolls. Fennel is also used to flavor candy, desserts, and soup. The oil of fennel is used in medicine, soaps and perfume.   I. H. S.

Fer de lance see Snakes

Fermentation Fermentation is the oxidation of ORGANIC COMPOUNDS in the absence of gaseous oxygen. It may be done by certain living organisms (YEAST, BACTERIA, MOLD) or by ENZYMES.

Fermi, Enrico (FERR-me, en-REE-koh) (1901-1954) Fermi was an Italian physicist who investigated the basic structure of the atomic nucleus. He received the 1938 Nobel Prize for physics for making a new radioactive element by neutron bombardment.

He was a pioneer in the study of nuclear fission (breaking of atoms into parts). He was largely responsible for the achievement of the nuclear chain reaction on December 2, 1942, at the University of Chicago, which made possible the first atomic bomb.

Born in Rome, Fermi studied and taught in Italy. He earned his doctorate from the University of Pisa and later taught at the universities of Florence and Rome, where he made his NOBEL PRIZE discovery. After receiving the Prize in Stockholm, he came to the United States instead of returning to Fascist-controlled Italy. He was professor of physics at Columbia University before he came to the University of Chicago to work on the atomic pile. He then became associate director of Los Alamos Laboratory, where the atomic bombs were tested. In 1946, he received the Congressional Medal for Merit and returned to Chicago as a member of the Institute for Basic Research.   C. L. K.

Fermi was largely responsible for the first controlled nuclear chain reaction. It took place on December 2, 1942, at Stagg Field of the University of Chicago

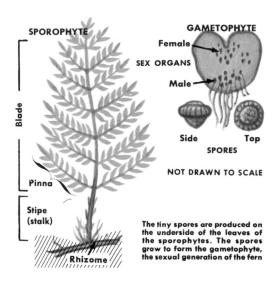

SPOROPHYTE   GAMETOPHYTE

Blade

Pinna

Stipe (stalk)

Rhizome

Female

SEX ORGANS

Male

Side   Top
SPORES

NOT DRAWN TO SCALE

The tiny spores are produced on the underside of the leaves of the sporophytes. The spores grow to form the gametophyte, the sexual generation of the fern

James P. Rowan

Young fern leaves are shaped like the head of a fiddle.

Fermium Fermium is a RARE-EARTH ELEMENT discovered in 1953. During test explosions of NUCLEAR ENERGY materials over a Pacific island, unmanned airplanes were sent through the radioactive clouds. These planes collected samples which, when tested, showed the presence of fermium.

Later, fermium was made in cyclotrons and in reactors in the laboratories at Argonne, Los Alamos, and the University of California. There are ten known isotopes of fermium. The isotope with the longest half-life is fermium 257, with a half-life of 80 days.

Fermium has the atomic number 100. Its symbol is Fm. Little is known about its chemical properties. Fermium oxide has been studied and shows a similarity to the oxide of the long-known element ERBIUM.

D.A.B.

SEE ALSO: ACTINIDE SERIES, ATOM, ELEMENTS

Ferns Ferns are members of the highest division of the plant kingdom. These plants, with their well-developed roots, and efficient water and food conducting systems, have become an important plant in many parts of the earth. Ferns grow in a variety of places, but most species prefer a moist, shady habitat.

Ferns are usually PERENNIAL with horizontal, underground stems—*rhizomes*—

which develop new fronds each year. The young leaves unroll at the tip, making the young plant look much like the head of a fiddle. The veins of the leaves branch into two almost equal forks which may unite to form a network of veins. The leaves are usually very irregular in outline, although, in a few species, they may be more regular.

Asexual reproduction in ferns is by SPORE FORMATION. These may develop on a separate frond, *sporophyll,* or they may be on the under side of regular leaves. Spores are produced in organs (*sporangia*) which are clustered together in groups known as *sori.* When a spore germinates it produces a *gametophyte* (the sexual generation). This is a small, flattened, heart-shaped structure which bears the male and female sex organs, *antheridia* and *archegonia.* When the moisture is right, the mature antheridia rupture, permitting the motile sperm cells to swim into the archegonia to fertilize the egg cells. The sporophyte generation develops from the fertilized egg.

Like the MOSSES, the ferns are excellent examples of the ALTERNATION OF GENERATIONS. In the ferns, however, the sporophyte is the important and familiar generation.

Ferns are a very old group of plants dating back to the Devonian period. They were the dominant plants of the MESOZOIC ERA. However, today the seed plants are more important.   M. D. F.

SEE ALSO: PLANTS, CLASSIFICATION OF

Ferret see Weasel

Fertile see Nuclear science glossary

✳ THINGS TO DO

GROWING TWO GENERATIONS OF THE FERN CYCLE

1 The fern (sporophyte generation) will thrive well in a bog terrarium. (See the Terrarium article for making it.)

2 Have the new home established before you go fern hunting. Ferns are found in wooded areas along the banks of streams or in a marshy environment.

3 Dig up the plant, being sure the entire underground stem is taken with it. Wrap it in wet newspaper and transfer the plants to the terrarium.

4 Keep the terrarium in a north window and water frequently.

5 To grow the second generation, the gametophyte, wait until the spores appear on the underside of the fronds. Tap the compound leaf over a sheet of paper and the spores will fall off.

6 Fill a pot with soil and peat moss. Put a layer of sand on top.

7 Pour boiling water over the whole mixture and the container to destroy any bacteria or mold spores which will attack the germinating fern spores, and let it cool.

8 Sprinkle the spores on the sand, cover the pot with clear glass, and set the pot in a saucer in order to water from the bottom.

9 In several weeks the spores will develop into minute heart-shaped gametophyte plants. This plant produces eggs and sperms. When a sperm fertilizes an egg, a small fern sporophyte will grow out of this plant. When it is several inches tall transfer it to the bog terrarium.

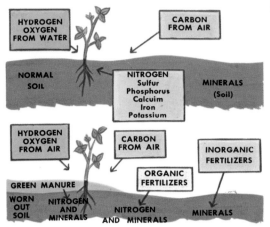

Fertilizers put food for plants back in the soil

Fertilization Fertilization is the union of male and female gametes (the sperm and egg) to form a single cell from which a new individual develops.

SEE: EMBRYOLOGY, REPRODUCTIVE SYSTEMS

Fertilizer This material is put into the soil to build up the MINERAL content. Homemade fertilizer may be manure or a compost made from decayed plant parts. Commercial fertilizer is a scientifically prepared mixture. Each year plants use up these important organic substances. They are needed to keep soil fertile.

The essential chemical elements are CARBON, HYDROGEN, OXYGEN, PHOSPHOROUS, SULFUR, MAGNESIUM, CALCIUM, NITROGEN and POTASSIUM. The plant gets the first three elements from air and water. The last six must be taken from the soil. Nitrogen is the most important and may be applied as nitrate, ammonia, tankage, or urea. Commercially complete fertilizer may be marked 4-12-4. It contains 4 percent nitrogen, 12 percent phosphorous, and 4 percent potassium.

Plants need tiny amounts of trace elements such as iron, copper, zinc, chlorine, and boron. Too much will kill them. A plant does not know how to select or when to stop absorbing.

Each mineral in the fertilizers is used by a particular part of the plant. Plants are given radioactive material. With a Geiger counter it can be traced. Phosphorous goes to the developing fruits. Magnesium is part of the chlorophyll molecule.   H. J. C.

SEE ALSO: AGRICULTURE, NITROGEN CYCLE

Fetus (FEE-tuhs) A fetus is an unborn mammal in the last stages of development within the mother's body. In man, the new individual, or baby, is classed as an embryo for the first three months of existence in the uterus. It is a fetus from then until born.

SEE: EMBRYOLOGY, MAMMALIA, PREGNANCY

Fever When a person's temperature rises above the normal temperature of 98.6 degrees F. (37° C.), fever is present. It is a symptom of infection in the body. The heat of fever is one method the body uses to help overcome the infection.

Loss of appetite and a chill usually accompany the beginning of a fever. As the temperature rises, the patient becomes hot and thirsty and may have a headache. Pathologists consider rising fever to be the result of toxins of the infection acting on the heat centers of the brain. As the infection subsides, the body temperature returns to normal and the patient rests more easily. Fever can often be reduced with ASPIRIN, but the infection causing it should be diagnosed and treated by a physician.   P.G.B.

SEE ALSO: MEDICINE, PATHOLOGY

Fiber A fiber is a thin thread-like strand. In plants, it is either a thin root or a long thin cell. In animals, a fiber is a long, thin strand which makes up part of the CONNECTIVE TISSUE, MUSCLE TISSUE, and nerve tissues in the body.

SEE: ECONOMIC BOTANY, NERVE CELL

Enlargements of wool fibers (left) and cotton fibers (right)

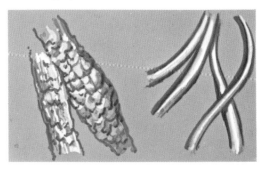

Photo-micrograph by National Teaching Aids, Inc.

Yellow elastic fibers in the trachea intertwine. The cells lie outside the fibers. The magnified cross-section (left) shows: A—air passage; B—lining; C—fibrous tissue; D—cartilage ring

Fibiger, Johannes Andreas (1867-1928) He was a Danish physician and professor of pathological anatomy who was one of the early CANCER researchers. He was awarded the 1928 NOBEL PRIZE in physiology and medicine.

His first cancer research began in 1913. In his later research he was able to induce what he thought to be a stomach cancer in rats by feeding them cockroaches infested with a certain species of West Indies roundworm. Upon examination of the test animals, he noted that tumors developed from irritation in their stomachs. It was later noted that the test animals lacked vitamin A and that a deficiency of this can cause injury to organs and tissue. Although the tumors in the rats were not cancerous, his later experiments provided evidence that cancer can originate as a result of parasites.   P.P.S.

Fibrin and fibrinogen see Blood, Circulatory system

Fibrous tissue Fibrous tissue helps to hold the internal organs and bones in place. It is a type of CONNECTIVE TISSUE. Fibrous tissue is made of white or yellow fibers and scattered cells. The cells make the fibers which are laid down outside the cell bodies.

The *yellow* elastic fibers are usually found where there is continuous but varying STRESS. Numerous branching yellow elastic fibers lie parallel to each other in the walls of the air tubes (RESPIRATORY SYSTEM) and in the vocal chords.

The *white* fibers are found in *ligaments,* which attach bones to bones, and in *tendons,* which attach muscles to bones. The fibers may be arranged in parallels, as in tendons, or interlaced in a membrane, as in the ligament covering JOINTS.

The Achilles tendon, attaching the calf muscle of the leg to the heel, is called this because Achilles, the mythical hero, was held by the heels when dipped in the river Styx to make him invulnerable. Later, a wound in the heel killed him.   E.M.S.

SEE ALSO: HISTOLOGY, MUSCLE TISSUE, SKELETON

Fibula see Skeleton

Field, Cyrus West (1819-1892) Cyrus Field was an American business man who, in 1854, organized the New York, Newfoundland and London Telegraph Company to lay trans-Atlantic cable. After three unsuccessful attempts, the cable was finally laid in July, 1866.

In 1854 he organized two companies in order to lay a cable across the Atlantic Ocean. A complete cable was laid between July 7 and August 5, 1858, and operated for three weeks. Queen Victoria sent a TELEGRAPH message across the Atlantic to President James Buchanan, and the world rejoiced. However, the insulation failed, and the project had to be abandoned.

In 1866 Field chartered the *Great Eastern,* and finally laid a successful cable. He was awarded a gold medal by Congress, and he received many honors.

During the last twenty-seven years of his life Field helped lay submarine cables to other parts of the world. He also was president of the New York Elevated Railroad Company for three years. Then he organized the Wabash Railroad.   D.H.J.

Fig tree and varieties of the fruit

Fig   The fig is a small tree or shrub which has been grown for over 4000 years. It originally came from Arabia. The pear-shaped fruit is not the true fruit of the tree. It is a hollow receptacle that is the swollen upper end of the flower stalk. Tiny flowers line the inside of this structure. They develop into small fruits called *achenes*.

There are several species of figs. The *golden fig* is an epiphyte. It starts its growth on another tree, sends out air roots, and finally grows downward until it anchors itself into the soil. During this process the host tree dies.

The *San Pedro fig* is grown in California and two crops of fruit are produced each year. The *common fig* lacks male flowers so the fruit matures seedless. Development of fruit without POLLINATION is called *parthenocarpy*.

Until the fruit growers in California learned about a particular *fig wasp,* they had little success raising the *Smyrna fig.* This tree has only female flowers. It needs the small female wasp which inhabits fruit of the wild *caprifig.* The insect carries the pollen from a male flower on this species to the female flower on the Smyrna fig. This process is called *caprification.*   H. J. C.

Filaria (fih-LAIR-ee-uh) A filaria is a long thread-like worm. It lives in the bodies of other animals. This means it is a *parasite*. The adults are found in the tissues of vertebrate animals. After the larvae develop, they cannot become adults unless part of their lives are spent within the bodies of insects. Most filariae are found in tropical countries.

One species of filaria lives in the lymph glands of man and may produce a disease called *elephantiasis*. It is so named because in a heavy infection (infestation) the arms, legs and other parts of the body swell to an enormous size. This probably happens because the lymph passages become blocked.

This species has an interesting life cycle. The adult worms are 2 to 4 inches (5.08 to 10.16 centimeters) long and they live inside human beings. The females give birth to larvae so small that one must view them under a microscope. These larvae find their way into the blood stream. During the day they live in the lungs and larger blood vessels. At night they move to the blood vessels of the skin. This increases their chances of being sucked up by night-feeding mosquitos. In places where the mosquitos feed during the day, the time of the larvae's day-night migration is reversed. Unless they are sucked up by mosquitos, the larvae cannot live.

Once inside the mosquito, the larvae pass from its stomach to its muscles where they change (metamorphose) and increase in size, before migrating back to the sucking tube (proboscis). When a person is bitten by an infected mosquito, the larvae enter the bloodstream of that person. They then pass to the lymph vessels and glands. There they coil up and mature into adults and the whole cycle starts again.   I. H. S.

SEE ALSO: METAMORPHOSIS

Filbert see Nuts

Filariae

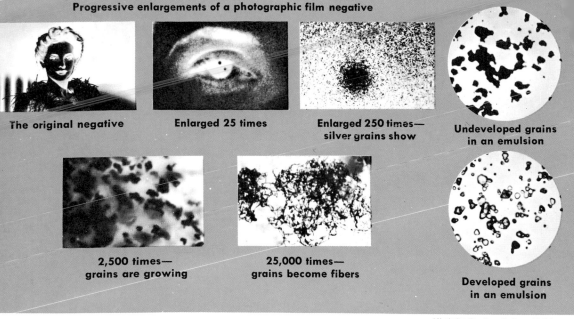

Progressive enlargements of a photographic film negative

The original negative

Enlarged 25 times

Enlarged 250 times—
silver grains show

Undeveloped grains
in an emulsion

2,500 times—
grains are growing

25,000 times—
grains become fibers

Developed grains
in an emulsion

All photos Courtesy Eastman Kodak

Film Film is a plastic-like material in thin sheets used for taking photographs. It is coated with special chemicals which are sensitive to light. These chemicals form an EMULSION, made up of gelatin and crystals of SILVER salts.

The process of film-making is an interesting one. The most important chemical used in the first step toward making film is silver nitrate. By placing silver ingots in nitric acid, the metal and acid combine and form crystals of silver nitrate.

The next step in the film preparation is to make an emulsion of silver bromide and gelatin. Silver nitrate, gelatin, and potassium bromide are mixed together in water. The potassium bromide and silver nitrate combine. Crystals of silver bromide are left in the gelatin. These particles are very sensitive to light and separate when light strikes them. When processed, this produces a *negative* which shows everything dark where the original scene was light, and light where everything was dark. Now the emulsion is complete and ready for use.

A film base must be prepared on which the emulsion will form a coating. Wood pulp or cotton is treated with ACETIC ACID to form cellulose acetate. It is then dissolved in a solvent and becomes a thick fluid which is called "dope." During a heating process the "dope" is turned into a very thin sheet. It is now transparent and ready to be coated with the emulsion. After coating, it is wound on metal spools and then packaged for sale.

Amateur photographers like to develop their own film into "positive" prints. Because the film is so light-sensitive, it must be developed in a completely dark room. The papers used for prints are coated with an emulsion quite like the one used on the film. After the print paper is placed against the negative under a white light, the print is then put through special chemical solutions and the image that appears has reproduced the lights and darks exactly as they were in the original scene photographed.

Color films reproduce a subject in its true life colors—red, green, and blue—from which all other colors come. There is also an emulsion backing on the film. When the pictures are developed, they are seen in the complementary colors which are exactly like those of the original subject. D. A. B.

SEE ALSO: CAMERA, PHOTOGRAPHY

Filter A filter is any object that can stop the passage of certain parts of a substance, while it lets the rest of the substance pass through it. A sieve is a filter. Sand and CHARCOAL are filters often used to remove impurities from drinking water.

In PHYSICS, a filter is a device that stops certain waves or rays (of sound, COLOR, or electricity) and lets others through.

SEE: CHEMISTRY, PURIFICATION, SOUND

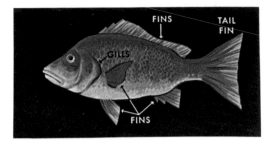

Fin A fin is the membranous organ attached to the body of a FISH. It corresponds to wings or limbs in other animals. It is used for locomotion, steering and balance in the water.
SEE: PISCES

Finch Finches belong to the order of perching birds (Passeriformes) in which three fifths of the known birds are placed. Finches are seedeaters, having the cone-shaped bill characteristic of the type. Bristles usually occur around the bill. They are not as migratory as insect-eating birds.

Most of the seedeaters belong in the family Fringillidae. This family includes some 700 species plus many subspecies and geographic races. Well-known members are the SPARROWS, GROSBEAKS, GOLDFINCHES, and BUNTINGS. Many finches are dull in color, particularly the females. The male purple finch is colorful but is more rose than purple. The house finch male is dull brownish like the female but has a bright red throat and head markings. In the western mountains are two species of rosy finches. One has a gray and the other a black crown. Darwin's classical studies were made upon adaptations in various finches of the Galápagos Islands.   J. C. K.

Purple finch

English sparrow

Fiord (FYOHRD) Fiords are ice-carved valleys which the sea has occupied after the glacial ice melted away. Fiords are long narrow valleys, steep-sided and often quite deep. They are formed as huge amounts of ice from continental glaciers or alpine glaciers scoop out natural valleys.

Fiords differ in many ways from other coastline features like natural harbors and bays. The shallowest part of a fiord is near the sea, while the deepest part is often well inland from the sea.

Some countries of the world are famous for the fiords that are part of their seacoast. Among these are the western coast of Alaska, parts of the British Isles, the northern coasts of Norway, and New Zealand.
SEE ALSO: GEOLOGY, RIVER   H.S.G.

Grosbeak

A fiord
Courtesy Society For Visual Education, Inc.

American Forest Products Industries, Inc.
Douglas fir, a false hemlock

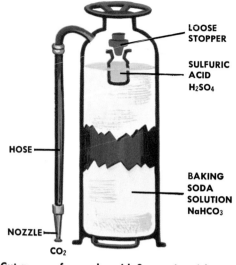

LOOSE STOPPER

SULFURIC ACID H_2SO_4

HOSE

BAKING SODA SOLUTION $NaHCO_3$

NOZZLE

CO_2

Cut-away of a soda-acid fire extinguisher

Fir Fir is any of the many cone-bearing, resinous, pyramid-shaped evergreens. The Norway SPRUCE fir can stand over 150 feet (45.72 meters). A well-known American species is the BALSAM fir. Because the wood is light, soft, and not strong, it is usually used to finish interiors and make boxes.

SEE: PINE, TREE

Fire When enough heat, fuel, and oxygen are present, a fire results. If any of these three things are lacking, there can be no fire. If any of the three are removed from a fire, it will stop burning and go out.

Fire is a chemical change that releases two kinds of ENERGY—heat and light. The release of energy takes place when the materials or some of the materials in the fuel combine with oxygen and form new materials.

Fires have always been very useful and necessary but can also be very destructive and harmful.   J. D. B.

SEE ALSO: COMBUSTION, FIRE EXTINGUISHER, OXIDATION

If any of the three components is removed, a fire cannot continue

HEAT   FUEL

OXYGEN

Fire extinguisher A fire extinguisher is a metal container which usually holds chemicals for putting out fires. When the chemicals mix and are sprayed on a fire, the fire goes out quickly. Fire extinguishers must be cleaned and inspected often, so they will be ready for use in case of an emergency.

The most widely used fire extinguisher is the CO_2 extinguisher. It is a tank of carbon dioxide under pressure. When released, the CO_2 cuts off the oxygen supply to the fire and it cannot continue burning.

The soda-acid type of fire extinguisher was once widely used. It contains a solution of bicarbonate of soda and water. There is a small bottle of SULFURIC ACID inside. To use the extinguisher one must turn it upside down. The stopper inside the sulfuric acid bottle comes loose. The acid pours out of the bottle and mixes with the chemicals to form CARBON DIOXIDE (CO_2). This carbon dioxide gas forces the chemicals through a hose attached to the container.

Another well-known extinguisher is the *foam* type. This is used mainly on gasoline or oil fires, because the foam smothers the flames of a burning liquid. These fire extinguishers contain a solution of SODIUM CARBONATE in one compartment and aluminum sulfate in another. When the extinguisher is inverted, the solutions mix into a foam which is forced through a hose.

✳ THINGS TO DO

MAKING A FIRE EXTINGUISHER

Materials: A pop bottle, soda straw, soda, vinegar, and clay.

1 **Form the clay around the end of the straw into a plug which can be used to cap the bottle. Fill the pop bottle half full of vinegar. Drop a tablespoon of baking soda into the bottle and immediately cap it with the clay-straw plug.**

2 **Have a small paper fire burning on a cookie sheet. Tilt the bottle, aiming the straw at the flames. What happened to the fire?**

3 **When vinegar and soda are combined a chemical change releases carbon dioxide. This gas is heavier than air, does not support combustion, and will smother the blaze.**

Automatic sprinklers are frequently used in department stores and factories where large areas must be protected against fires. Pipes which contain water under pressure are placed throughout the ceilings. Sprinkler heads, which have soft metal plugs in them, are set into the pipes every 8 to 10 feet (2.4 to 3 meters). If a fire breaks out in a room with this system, the plugs melt when the heat reaches 165° F. (73.9° C.). This opens the sprinklers and the water sprays out with great force. A bell rings until the water is shut off by the fire department. J.H.D.

Firearms see Weapons

Firefly see Beetles

First aid The care given to an injured or suddenly ill person before a doctor arrives is first aid. It is given *only* to prevent death or permanent disability. First aid care should not take the place of the doctor.

General directions that should be followed when a person is injured include:

1. A doctor should be called while first aid is being given.
2. The injured person must be kept lying down, his head level with the rest of his body unless he has a head injury. If he has a head injury, his head should be slightly raised.
3. An injured person *should not be moved,* except to remove him from fire, flood, smoke, or anything that would further endanger his life.
4. An injured person should be examined to see if emergency action is really necessary. If he is *not* in danger of bleeding to death, or is *not* suffocating, or has *not* been severely burned, or is *not* in shock, the untrained person should leave him alone.
5. An unconscious or semiconscious person should never be given anything to drink.
6. An injured person should be kept warm—not hot.
7. Other people should be kept away from the injured person.
8. An injured person should be reassured, not permitted to see his wounds, and kept comfortable until a doctor comes.

Shock can result from almost any injury. There is a sudden drop in blood pressure

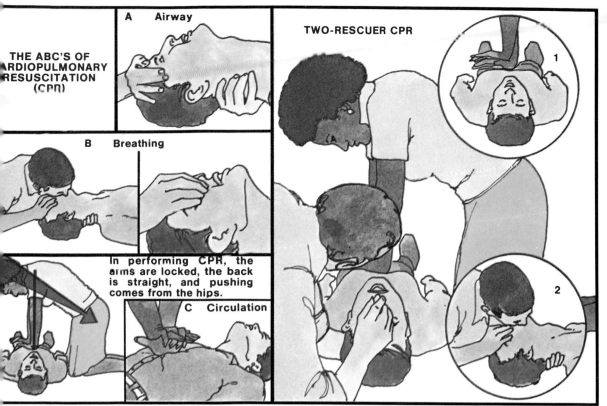

THE ABC'S OF CARDIOPULMONARY RESUSCITATION (CPR)

A   Airway

B   Breathing

In performing CPR, the arms are locked, the back is straight, and pushing comes from the hips.

C   Circulation

TWO-RESCUER CPR

1

2

In CPR, used when the heart stops beating, the rescuers both *compress the heart* (at a rate of 60 compressions per minute) and *inflate the lungs* with artificial respiration techniques (1 breath after every 5 compressions, with no stop in compressions). If a single rescuer is performing CPR, he or she compresses the heart 5 times, and then inflates the lungs once. NOTE: Everyone should be instructed in these techniques by trained medical personnel.

and/or blood volume. If not promptly treated, it can result in death due to the lack of oxygen supply to the brain and other organs. A person in shock may have a pale face, cold sweat, weak, rapid pulse, and nausea. Victims should be placed on their back unless there is vomiting, in which case victims should be placed on their side. If conscious, the person may be given chips of ice to chew on.

Bleeding can be stopped by applying pressure. Place a clean pad over the wound and press down firmly. When bleeding is controlled, wrap the wound with a bandage or a clean cloth until medical attention can be gotten. Many experts now agree that a tourniquet should never be applied because of the damage a tourniquet can do. Keep constant pressure on a heavily bleeding wound until help arrives.

Burns may result in shock and infection. The pain may be relieved by immersing the burned area in cold water. Grease, oil, or anything a doctor would have to remove before treating the burn must *never* be used. The burned area may be covered with sterile gauze if no doctor is available.

An ice bag should be applied to the area of a *fracture* to relieve pain. A person with possible fractures should not be moved except to prevent further injury. The broken bone must be splinted before moving. A board, a thick bundle of newspapers, or even a pillow can be used. The splint should be tied firmly in place above and below the break. If the neck or back is injured, the victim *must not be moved*.

Poisoning requires emergency treatment as soon as the doctor or a Poison Control Center is called. Once the poison is identified, the person can be made to vomit (unless the poisoning is from an alkali, like lye, or a volatile hydrocarbon, like kerosene) using salt water, mustard water, or syrup of ipecac. If the proper antidote is known (baking soda for acids, vinegar for alkalis), it should be given. If unknown, activated charcoal in water is given.

Suffocation can result from pressure on the neck or chest, an electric shock, or swallowing liquids, smoke or, especially in children, small hard objects. The cause of suffocation must first be removed, for example, by taking the victim out of a smoke-filled room. ARTIFICIAL RESPIRATION and/or CPR should then be applied until the victim resumes breathing or is pronounced dead.

Cuts and lacerations should be thoroughly cleaned with soap and water. A large cut

685

should be seen by a doctor. Puncture wounds should *always* be seen by a doctor because of the danger of tetanus infection.

Foreign bodies in the eye may be washed out with a solution of one teaspoon (.18 milliliter) of baking soda in a glass of warm, sterilized water. Foreign bodies in the nose or ear should be removed by a physician. If the victim is choking due to a foreign body in the throat, it should be expelled by quick upward thrusts to the abdomen (the Heimlich Choke Maneuver).

Animal bites should be cleaned with soap and water. A doctor should see the victim as soon as possible. The animal should be kept under observation for rabies.

Snake bites require special care. With the victim lying down, a band should be tied between the bite and the heart, to slow down the spread of the poison. Using a sterilized knife, crisscross cuts about ¼ inch (.64 centimeter) long should be made through each fang mark. Sucking venom out of the bite is hardly done because injections of "antivenom" are preferable.

A *strain* is an over-stretching of muscles or other bodily tissues. A *sprain* is an injury to a joint or a tearing of muscles, ligaments, or tendons. There may be bleeding into a joint producing a black and blue mark. There is no fracture to a bone or dislocation of a joint. A sprain is best treated by cold applications at first and later by heat. A strain is soothed by heat. Both should be rested.

Sunstroke, heat exhaustion, and heat cramps are due to exposure to excessive temperatures. Heat cramps and heat exhaustion require salt replacement of lost perspiration. Sunstroke requires cooling by cold water. All require removal from the environment.

Frostbite victims should be brought indoors and the frozen area immediately thawed with tepid (not hot) water. Snow should *not* be used, and the area should *not* be massaged. Heat or massage can burn or damage the frost-bitten skin.   J.D.B./E.S.S.

SEE ALSO: ARTIFICIAL RESPIRATION, HEIMLICH CHOKE MANEUVER

Fischer, Emil (1852-1919) He was a German organic chemist who was a pioneer in the development of synthetic sugar. He received the 1902 NOBEL PRIZE in chemistry His other

research dealt with the PURINE group, the polypeptides and peptides.

Fisher, using new reagents and techniques, made great progress in explaining the molecular structure of many compounds. Almost all knowledge of purines is attributed to the work of Fischer. In the sugar group, he synthesized FRUCTOSE, GLUCOSE, and many other substances. He established procedures for distinguishing formulas for these sugars, and initiated study into the nature, properties, and reactions of substances which bring about fermentation. His research lead to the foundation of enzyme chemistry.   P.P.S.

Fischer, Hans (1881-1945) He was a German biochemist who was awarded the NOBEL PRIZE for his research with the composition of *hemin* and CHLOROPHYLL. His work in the chemistry of blood indicated a common ancestry with chlorophyll.

Fischer's research into the composition of hemin and chlorophyll led to the eventual synthesis of hemin (the crystalline product of hemoglobin). This was possible because he was able to isolate a section of hemin intact. Once its structure was identified, it became possible to synthesize hemin from simpler organic materials with better known and less complicated structure. At the time of his death, Fischer was very close to the synthesis of chlorophyll. He had also studied the yellow pigment *carotene,* a forerunner of vitamin A, and the *porphyrins* (derivatives of chlorophyll and hemoglobin). He realized that they were widely distributed in nature and secreted by man in certain diseases.   P.P.S.

Fish Not all the animals that live in water are fish. Tadpoles, frogs, and newts, for instance, spend part of their lives in water. But they are amphibians, not fish. Some snakes and other reptiles live partly in water, too. Seals and whales are warm-blooded mammals. Crayfish, starfish and jellyfish are not true fish. Sharks, lampreys, hagfish, and bony fish are all true fish.

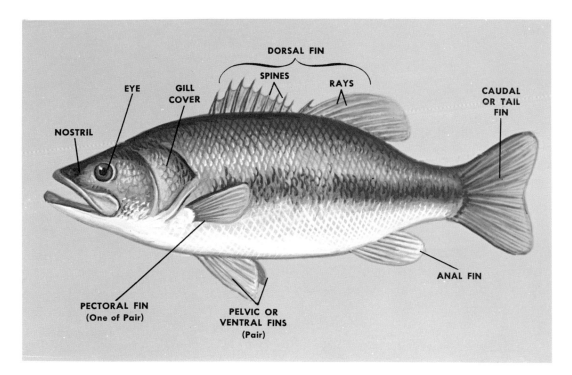

DORSAL FIN
SPINES
RAYS
EYE
GILL COVER
CAUDAL OR TAIL FIN
NOSTRIL
ANAL FIN
PECTORAL FIN
(One of Pair)
PELVIC OR VENTRAL FINS
(Pair)

1—Fresh water fish in Lake Michigan
2—Marine habitat group off the coast of Texas in the Gulf of Mexico
3—Marine shore group off the Maine coast

"Fish" is a general name that many people give to vertebrates that live in water, breathe through gills, and swim with fins. Modern scientists, however, usually make a separate grouping for the jawless and gill-less fish, such as lampreys and hagfish. These animals look somewhat like eels. This group is called *Agnatha,* or sometimes *Cyclostomata.*

SHARKS and other cartilaginous fish are called *Chondrichthyes.* These animals do not have a true bony skeleton. Their skeletons are made of CARTILAGE, a firm, flexible substance. The cartilaginous group of fish may have a tough skin with toothlike scales. They do not have ribs, lungs, an air bladder, or true gill covers. Their fins are supported by cartilaginous fin rays. Some fish have bony, jointed fin rays.

The differences between cartilaginous fish and bony fish (the *teleosts*) have special significance in evolutionary studies.   C. L. K.

SEE ALSO: PISCES

Fish hawk see Osprey

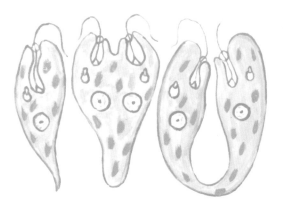

Fission of Euglena

Fittonia

Fission (FISH-uhn) In BIOLOGY, fission is the splitting of an organism (such as bacteria) into two or more parts, each of which becomes a complete organism. Fission is a form of asexual reproduction because the new organism is created without any union of the male and female sex cells, or gametes.

In physics, fission is the splitting of the nucleus of an atom.
SEE: NUCLEAR SCIENCE; REPRODUCTION, ASEXUAL

Fissionable see Nuclear science glossary

Fittonia (fih-TONE-yuh) Fittonia is a tropical, PERENNIAL plant which is raised mainly for its hairy and beautifully veined foliage. Fittonias will grow in shade and in places that most other plants will not grow. They are useful as low or creeping foliage plants. They should be planted in pots, with equal parts of sand, leaf-mold and loam.

Fittonias have small, two-lipped flowers which are hidden by their leaves. Some fittonias have dark green leaves which are veined with red. Others have white-veined leaves. The largest fittonia is about a foot (.3 meter) in height and has red-veined, short-pointed leaves.   M.R.L.
SEE ALSO: PLANTS, TROPICAL

Fjord see Fiord

Flagella (fluh-JELL-uh) In BOTANY, flagella are thin thread-like roots or runners. In BIOLOGY, flagella are whip-like appendages, or parts, on certain organisms (some PROTOZOA and BACTERIA) by which the organism moves.
SEE: ANIMALS, CLASSIFICATION OF

Flame see Combustion

Flamingo In spite of its deep voice and height of nearly 5 feet (1.52 meters), the flamingo is a very timid bird. Its long legs are like the heron's, but its feet are webbed like a duck's. When feeding, the flamingo buries its curved bill upside down in water or mud. Its food, seeds and small water animals, are strained out by the fine comb-like edges at the side of the bill.

Flamingos
Courtesy Society For Visual Education, Inc.

This bird lives along coastal areas or shallow lagoons of tropical regions. At one time, the demand for the beautiful scarlet plumage of the American flamingo nearly caused its extinction. It is now protected by law. In Europe and Africa, the flamingo is usually white. Other species of flamingo may be pink or white with black wing quills.

The flamingo builds its nest of mud, less than a foot (.3 meter) high and a foot wide. It lays one or two white eggs in a shallow depression. Both parents share the thirty-day incubation period.   J.A.D.

SEE ALSO: BIRD, HERON

Flatfish Flatfish are FISH that have compressed, or flat, bodies. As adults, they have both eyes on the same side of the head. The FLOUNDER and HALIBUT are kinds of flatfish.

Flatworm see Planaria, Platyhelminthes

Flax see Linen

Flea Fleas are jumping INSECTS (order Syphonaptera). They are bloodsucking PARASITES that live on the bodies of birds and mammals. They commonly infest rats, dogs, cats, and man. Fleas are small with flattened sides, sucking mouthparts, long hind legs, and no wings. They can jump about fifty times their own length.

There are five to seven families of fleas. The family Pulicidae includes the common dog, cat, and human flea. These fleas have eyes. Species in another family live on rodents. Many of these lack eyes. The common rat flea is an intermediate host for a human tapeworm and transmits the disease bubonic plague.   J. C. K.

SEE ALSO: INSECTA, METAMORPHOSIS

Fleming, Sir Alexander (1881-1955) Sir Alexander Fleming was the British bacteriologist who discovered the green mold *Penicillium notatum* from which PENICILLIN is made.

In 1922, Fleming found "a substance present in the tissues and secretion of the body which is capable of rapidly dissolving certain bacteria." As it resembled an enzyme and was able to *lyse* (dissolve) cells, he called it "lysozyme." Lysozyme is widely used in BACTERIOLOGY.

In 1928, a green mold ruined one of Fleming's bacteria cultures. He found that this mold did not damage the white blood cells of test mice. He had his bacterium-fighter, but medical researchers were more interested in the new SULFA DRUGS. When the inadequacies of sulfa were discovered, Sir Florey, an Oxford University pathologist, remembered Fleming's green mold. With his wife, also a physician, and Dr. Ernst Chain, he developed natural penicillin, the first major ANTIBIOTIC.

For his pioneering work in bacteriology, Fleming was knighted in 1944. He shared the 1945 NOBEL PRIZE for medicine with Sir Howard Florey and Dr. Chain.   D.H.J.

Fleming, Sir Sanford (1827-1915) He was engineer-in-chief of surveys for the Canadian Railway. He is best known for his encouragement of the 24-hour-day system of time keeping and the establishment of time zones.

Fleming, after supervising railway construction throughout eastern Canada, led an expedition west to survey the route later used by the Canadian Pacific Railway.

In 1874, there were no standardized time zones in the United States and Canada, and a serious problem of time differences affected the railways of both countries. After ten years of talk, Fleming in Canada and Charles F. Dowd in the United States got railway managers to accept the present standard time-zone system.   P.P.S.

Flesh Flesh is the soft part of an animal body, such as muscle, fat, and skin. Animals that eat the flesh of other animals are called *carnivores*.

The flicker is a climbing bird

Flicker Flickers are a type of woodpecker belonging to the family Picidae. The northern species have pointed straight bills, large heads, and short legs. The gray black-barred body has a lighter-spotted breast, a white rump, and a gray crown with a red band across the back of the neck.

Other features are a black throat crescent and broad black bands forming a moustache leading down from the base of the bill. In the northern flicker the underwings and feather shafts are yellow. In the western species, these parts are red. The two species may hybridize or mate.

Feet are unusual with two toes directed forward and two backward. The feet, plus the stiff sharp tail, are adaptations for climbing on tree trunks. Flickers, however, do more ground feeding than other woodpeckers. They eat ants whenever possible.

These birds dig their nests in a dead tree and lay six to eight white eggs. Both parents incubate and feed them.   J. C. K.

Flight, principles of Through the ages, man has watched the birds and dreamed of flying. In every age "scientists" devised flying machines. The earliest recorded model, based on bird flight, dates back to 400 B.C.

Birds fly by moving their wings down and up. During the downstroke, the wing moves forward and down with a twisting motion. The BIRD then moves forward rapidly. During the upstroke, the wings move backward, but the bird still moves forward because of momentum gained on the downstroke. The tips of the wings move much more rapidly than the point at which they are attached to the body of the bird.

Many of the early flying machines were *ornithopters*. An ornithopter is an aircraft which has wings that try to duplicate the movement of those of a bird in flight. Although small-scale models have been built and flown successfully, the mechanical problems in making the conversion from a model to a full-size aircraft have not been solved.

LIFT AND GRAVITY

The wings of fixed-wing aircraft are shaped so that air flowing over the top of the wing moves faster than air moving across the bottom. The faster moving air has less pressure, and the greater pressure on the bottom of the wing makes it rise. This upward push is called *lift*.

Lift may be increased by increasing the speed of the aircraft or the angle at which the wing is moved through the air. This *angle of attack* is increased by raising the nose of the aircraft. If the angle of attack becomes too great, the flow of air over the top of the wing will start to swirl and burble, causing a loss of lift called a *stall*. The angle of attack must then be reduced, and the speed of the wing through the air increased, to restore the lift necessary to maintain flight.

Most aircraft have *flaps*, trailing edge sections of their wings hinged to lower downward. This changes the shape of the wing airfoil to provide greater lift at low speeds for safer take-offs and landings.

Lift must be greater than the force of *gravity* acting upon the aircraft for it to leave the ground and climb into the atmosphere. In straight and level flight, lift and gravity are in exact balance. When gravity is greater than lift, the aircraft will descend.

THRUST AND DRAG

The aircraft powerplant provides the force called *thrust* which propels the vehicle

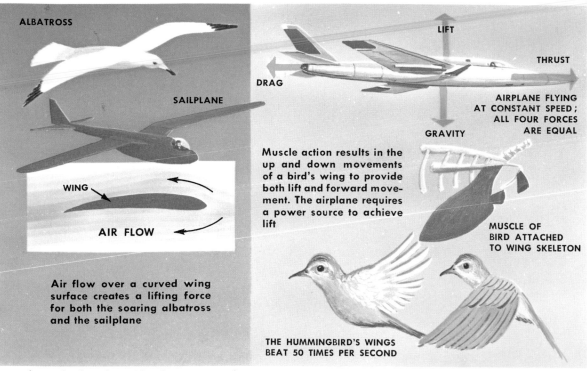

ALBATROSS

SAILPLANE

LIFT

THRUST

DRAG

AIRPLANE FLYING
AT CONSTANT SPEED;
ALL FOUR FORCES
ARE EQUAL

GRAVITY

WING

AIR FLOW

Muscle action results in the
up and down movements
of a bird's wing to provide
both lift and forward movement. The airplane requires
a power source to achieve
lift

MUSCLE OF
BIRD ATTACHED
TO WING SKELETON

Air flow over a curved wing
surface creates a lifting force
for both the soaring albatross
and the sailplane

THE HUMMINGBIRD'S WINGS
BEAT 50 TIMES PER SECOND

through the air. This thrust must be great enough to start the aircraft in motion and to build up sufficient speed to create lift for flight. Acting against thrust is another force called *drag*. This force is created by the resistance of the air to the forward movement of the aircraft.

All exposed parts of the aircraft create drag. Designers attempt to streamline the entire aircraft to give it a shape which will offer the least resistance to the air. Even small bumps and irregularities in the surface of the aircraft cause a form of drag called *skin friction*. If thrust exceeds drag, the aircraft accelerates. If it is less than the drag, the aircraft slows down.

An aircraft in level flight at a constant speed and altitude requires that lift must equal gravity and thrust must equal drag.

CONTROLS

Aircraft are designed with controls to regulate *lift, pitch* (raising or lowering nose), *roll* (angular motion of wings), and *yaw* (side-to-side motion of nose). The pilot's *throttle* regulates the amount of thrust produced by the engine. This affects the speed of the aircraft and its corresponding lift. *Elevators,* located on the horizontal stabilizer, raise or lower the position of the nose of the aircraft around the axis of pitch. Forward pressure on the control wheel (or *stick*) lowers the nose; a backward movement raises it. The airspeed and attitude of climbing and descending flight are governed by coordinating the throttle and elevator

controls. In a gliding descent, for example, thrust is reduced but the desired airspeed is maintained by lowering the nose.

The *ailerons* control the movement of the aircraft around the axis of roll. Pressure to the left on the control stick results in lowering the left wing and raising the right.

The pilot exerts right or left foot pressure on the rudder pedals to control the aircraft movement about the *axis of yaw*. This rudder action is similar to that of a ship and swings the nose of the aircraft right or left.

Control pressures are seldom used separately. The simplest maneuver needs coordination of all three pressures. A simple turn to the right requires coordinated pressures on ailerons, rudder, and elevator.

Aircraft are designed to be properly balanced for flight—to have *inherent stability*—so that the aircraft will tend to fly straight and level with a minimum of control by the pilot. Variations in weight location, speeds, climbing, gliding, and many other factors require the pilot to exert corrective pressures on the controls. To relieve the pilot of this constant control pressure, aircraft are provided with *trim tabs,* small, hinged control surfaces on the main control surfaces. They can be adjusted from the cockpit to balance the forces on the controls.   R. J. J.

SEE ALSO: AIRCRAFT, AIRPLANE, INSTRUMENT LANDING SYSTEM, INSTRUMENT PANEL

Flightless birds see Birds, flightless

Flint see Rocks

U.S. Department of Agriculture

A dairy farm flooded by the Columbia River

Floe see Iceberg

Flood A flood is the overflowing of water onto land that is normally dry. Most floods occur in spring when heavy rains and melting snow bring more water to streams and rivers than their channels can carry. The extra water flows over surrounding land.

The flooded part of the river valley is called a *flood plain*. Because young rivers have narrow flood plains, their floods do not cover much territory. Mature and older rivers, such as the Nile or the Mississippi, have gradually developed broad flood plains, so their floods cover larger areas.

A single heavy downpour in the narrow valley of a young mountain stream may turn it into a violent torrent within a few hours. This is called a *flash flood*. Great rivers, as the lower course of the Missouri, Ohio and the Mississippi, never have flash floods. Their floods are usually the result of many days of rainfall over large areas.

There are several methods of flood prevention. One of these is to build *levees* of sandbags, concrete, or other materials. The levees keep the river from overflowing the banks. Another way is to reduce the amount of water flowing in a river. This is done by building a system of *dams* on the river and its tributaries. The danger of a flood can also be reduced by restoring the natural vegetation that men have destroyed. Grasslands and forests near streams hold water back and are vital to flood control.   C.L.K.

SEE ALSO: DAM, RIVER

Flora Flora is the plant population of a particular place or of a certain period of time. The term usually covers all plants of a given region, or during a geological period.

SEE: GEOGRAPHY, GEOLOGIC TIME TABLE, PALEONTOLOGY, PLANT

Flory, Paul J. (1910-1985) He is a scientist who received the 1974 NOBEL PRIZE in chemistry. His research developed the techniques now generally used in the study of *polymers*.

Dr. Flory studied polymers, long-chain molecules that form through the linkage of many smaller molecules. Polymers occur in many important commercial compounds like paint and plastics. Flory also discovered that for each polymer there is a specific temperature which defines the length that a molecular chain can reach. This discovery was later named the *Flory temperature*.   P.P.S.

Flotation In the flotation process, crude ORE is ground to a fine powder and placed in a water-oil solution which is stirred to a froth. The lighter materials float off on the froth; heavier materials settle out.

Flounder Flounder, halibut, turbot, and sole are all flatfish. They are flattened from side to side and have one long spineless dorsal FIN and a similar anal fin. They swim on one side with both eyes on the upper side.

As young flounders mature they list to one side. One eye migrates across the "forehead" to a position next to the other. The swim bladder disappears, the mouth may become twisted, and the underside of the body paler. The pectoral fin on the underside may be smaller.   J.C.K.

SEE ALSO: PISCES

Starry flounder

Chicago Natural History Museum

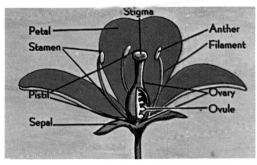

Longitudinal-section of a typical flower

Flour

Flour This is the endosperm or stored starch milled from grains. Graham flour is made from the whole seed, whole wheat has part of the bran removed, and white flour lacks the seed coat and embryo.

SEE: CEREAL GRAINS

Flower

Flower A flower is the part of a plant which leads to the forming of fruits and seeds. It is a special stem with floral leaves. Only the highest group in the plant kingdom produces flowers. They vary in color, shape, size, number of parts, and in other features. The blooms on some plants are so tiny one needs a magnifying glass to see their parts. The rafflesia, which grows in tropical forests, has a flower which is 4 feet (1.22 meters) across.

A perfect, complete flower has the following structures. The flower stalk or pedicel has an enlarged end or receptacle. The outer floral ring or sepals are attached to it. Collectively the sepals are called the CALYX and serve as protection for the flower bud before it opens. They are often green and small. The second ring is composed of the petals or COROLLA. They are usually the brightly colored or white floral parts, and they attract insects and birds. Together the calyx and corolla are called the perianth. The STAMENS or male organs make up the third circle. Each one has a stalk or filament which holds an anther at its upper end. The anther has two halves, each producing many pollen grains. The PISTIL or female organ has three parts. The enlarged base is the ovary. A sim-

Petals, stamens and pistil are clearly seen in a dogtooth violet

ple ovary has one chamber or carpel while a compound ovary has two or more. Ovules, which contain the future seeds, are attached to the ovary wall. The style is an elongated tube extending out from the ovary. The end of it is enlarged to form a stigma which is often sticky and holds the pollen.

A complete flower has petals, sepals, stamens, and pistil. An incomplete flower has one or more of these missing. A perfect flower has both sex organs, while imperfect flowers are either male or female. A monoecious plant has imperfect blooms on the same plant, as in squash, walnut, and corn. Dioecious plants have sex structures on separate plants, as in willow, asparagus, and date palm. Coalescence is the fusion of flower parts. Legumes have fused stamens, petunias have fused petals, and pinks have fused sepals. Inflorescence is a flower cluster on the top of one stalk or pedicel. The tassel of corn is an inflorescence of male flowers. A COMPOSITE has ray and disk flowers together or alone. An umbel is a spray of flowers shaped like an umbrella. The catkin of willow is spikelike. These are all types of inflorescences.

Some flowers possess bracts which are

Most trees bear flowers

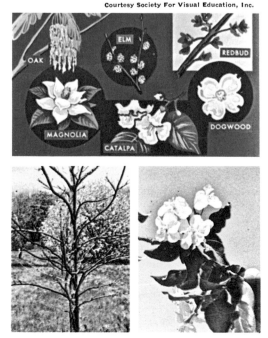

Flowers, or blossoms, come in as many varieties as there are flowering plants; for example (top row from left)—blue-eyed grass, a mountain meadow grass; butter-and-eggs, a plant requiring little water; Joshua, a desert tree; (bottom row from left) dandelions, a common wild flower; and trumpet creeper, a climbing vine

modified leaves or scales. The flowers of poinsettia are in the center of large red or white bracts. A spathe is a large single bract, as in calla lily, which is around a flower spike.

The purpose of flower parts is to reproduce the seeds. POLLINATION is the transfer of pollen or male cells to the stigma of the pistil. A pollen tube grows down the style. The sperm unites with the egg in the ovary. This is fertilization. The zygote grows into a seed and the ovary wall matures into the fruit. When this occurs the rest of the floral organs wither and drop off.

Recently plants are being grouped according to their response to the number of daylight hours needed for flowering. This is called *photoperiodism*. Short-day plants must have over 12 hours of darkness per day. They bloom in spring and fall. Long-day plants need over 12 hours of daylight and bloom in summer. The day-neutral do well anytime.

Growth hormones are now used extensively. *Florigen* is a plant hormone which as yet has not been isolated. Scientists believe it is the chemical that stimulates a bud to develop into a flower. Gibberellins are hormones which cause long-day plants to bloom. Auxins usually come from the embryo in the seed after pollination and cause the fruit to mature. Artificial parthenocarpy is done by spraying these growth hormones on unpollinated flowers causing them to produce seedless fruit. Maleic hydrasize is a chemical currently used to slow or stop plants from flowering. Floraculture is a rapidly growing science. H. J. C.
SEE ALSO: ANGIOSPERMS, FRUIT, POLLINATION, SEED

Fluid A fluid is a substance which is capable of flowing. All liquids and gases are fluids. Air is both a GAS and a fluid; water is both a LIQUID and a fluid.

SEE: SUBSTANCES, PROPERTIES OF

Fluke see Liver fluke, Platyhelminthes

Fluorescent light see Bulb, electric

Fluorine Fluorine is a pale greenish-yellow poisonous GAS. It has a strong odor and eats away almost any moist material. Fluorine will combine to some extent with all elements except helium, neon, and argon. It is one of the most chemically active elements. Its atomic number is 9, and its atomic weight 19.00. The symbol for fluorine is F.

The chief ores of fluorine are FLUORITE and CRYOLITE. Fluoride compounds are also found in sea water, and bones, nails, and teeth of animals.

It is the seventeenth most common element in the earth's crust.

Although fluorine is not rare, it required seventy-five years of experimenting by many scientists before fluorine was finally isolated in 1886 by H. Moissan. He obtained it by passing electricity through liquid hydrogen fluoride with potassium fluoride dissolved in it.

Fluorides are added to drinking water in cities throughout the United States and Canada. This process is called fluoridation, and it reduces tooth decay.

Fluorine is important as one of the elements which will combine with some of the "inert" elements, xenon, krypton, and radon—a chemical property which it shares directly only with oxygen. This discovery revolutionized chemical theory.

SEE ALSO: ELEMENTS

Fluorite (FLOO-uh-rite) Fluorite is a

MINERAL containing CALCIUM and FLUORINE. Fluorite is a transparent or translucent mineral, and is medium soft and brittle. Varieties are white, blue, green, violet, or red. Some pieces of fluorite change color as the light strikes them from different angles. They are called *fluorescent. Fluorspar* is a rock

The United States is the largest producer of fluorite. It is mined in Illinois, Kentucky, Colorado, and New Mexico. Canada and Spain also have large deposits.

Fluorite is used in steel-making to make a fluid slag. It is also used in making enamel for cooking utensils, and in making FREON, a refrigerator coolant.   J.K.L.

Fluorocarbons A fluorocarbon is an

organic compound that contains FLUORINE. Fluorocarbons are used in refrigerators and air conditioners. They are also used to make plastics.

Freon is a name used for a group of fluorocarbons. Freons are used in refrigeration and as a propellant in aerosol cans. There is very serious evidence that freons are capable of breaking down the earth's OZONE layer. Concerted efforts are being made to limit the use of freons.

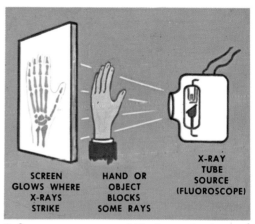

SCREEN GLOWS WHERE X-RAYS STRIKE | HAND OR OBJECT BLOCKS SOME RAYS | X-RAY TUBE SOURCE (FLUOROSCOPE)

A fluoroscope can reveal the inner structures of organisms and objects

The polymer of tetrafluorothene is the widely used plastic, Teflon.   A.J.H.

Fluoroscope When a person is ill, many instruments may be used in gathering the necessary information to make a proper diagnosis of the illness. The fluoroscope is one such instrument. It is especially useful because it allows the physician to observe instantly the bone structure and the internal organs of his patient. It also reveals foreign matter that may be present, as in the case of a baby swallowing a pin or other metal objects.

A fluoroscope reveals opaque or partially opaque images in the human body by passing X rays through the body.

The fluoroscope consists of two parts—an X-ray tube and a screen. The usual type of screen is made of cardboard covered with certain fluorescent substances such as barium plastino-cyanide, calcium tungstate or other CRYSTALS. The fluorescent substances change the invisible X-ray radiation into visible light. The screen is covered with lead glass.

The fluoroscope must be used in a darkened room. The patient stands in front of the X-ray tube. The fluorescent screen is placed over the part of the body to be examined. Invisible X-rays are passed through the patient's body. These rays are partially blocked by the bones and internal organs. As a result a shadow image of the organs under examination is cast on the screen.

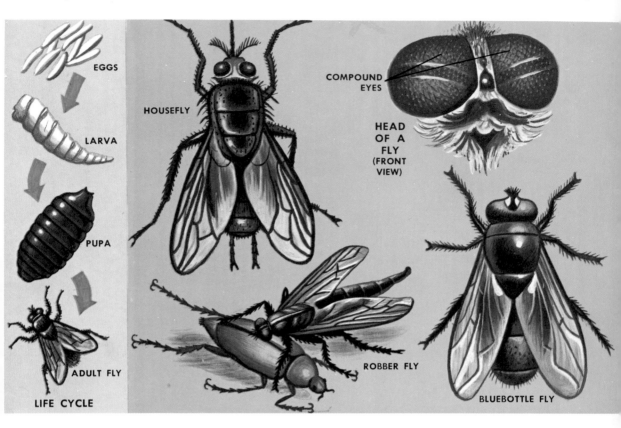

EGGS

LARVA

PUPA

ADULT FLY

LIFE CYCLE

HOUSEFLY

COMPOUND EYES

HEAD OF A FLY (FRONT VIEW)

ROBBER FLY

BLUEBOTTLE FLY

The thicker, more opaque organs cast darker shadows because fewer X rays are able to pass through them to show up on the fluorescent screen.

The fluoroscope has been especially useful in the detection of diseases of the LUNGS, the stomach, and the HEART. Besides its use in diagnosis, it is also useful as an aid to other medical procedures. By using the fluoroscope physicians are able to perform very tedious and difficult tasks, such as medicating hidden organs and removing small tumors without major surgery.

Today, some hospitals link their fluoroscope with a closed circuit television. This permits instant observation of the organs in a room other than the darkened X-ray room, giving a permanent record of the case. G. A. D.
SEE ALSO: MEDICINE, PATHOLOGY, X-RAY

Fly Flies are two-winged insects that breed in moist places. Butterflies, dragonflies, and damsel flies are not true flies because they have four wings, as do most other insects.

The *housefly* is the fly that people know best. It breeds in garbage and manure. It then carries the germs of typhoid, DYSENTERY, and cholera on its feet to the food and dishes of man. Proper disposal of refuse and filth and the use of certain chemicals cut down the number of houseflies.

Some flies are helpful to man in pollinating plants and eating other insects, but most flies are dangerous pests. The blood-sucking *tsetse fly* of Africa may carry the fatal SLEEPING SICKNESS. Tiny eye gnats and midges are flies that not only torment, but carry disease.

Warble flies and black flies are harmful to animals. The Mediterranean FRUIT FLY and the Hessian fly harm plants.

Over 85,000 species of flies have been classified and many more remain as yet unidentified. Varieties are found in all countries. The wingless crane fly has been seen on the surface of snow.

A fly has a shell-like exoskeleton. Modi-

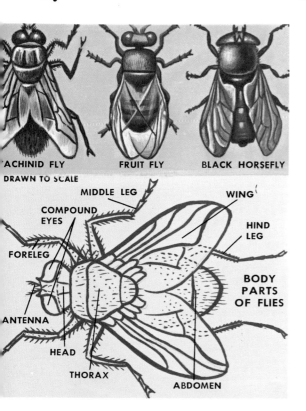

ACHINID FLY   FRUIT FLY   BLACK HORSEFLY

DRAWN TO SCALE

COMPOUND EYES · MIDDLE LEG · WING · HIND LEG · FORELEG · ANTENNA · HEAD · THORAX · ABDOMEN · BODY PARTS OF FLIES

Reproduction varies with the species. Houseflies lay over a hundred eggs at one time. Some species may lay only one egg and the tsetse fly lays none, but retains her eggs until the pupa stage. The fruit fly produces so many generations so rapidly that it is used in studies of heredity and evolution.

The eggs of the fly turn into slug-like *maggots,* or larvae. The maggots become pupae which soon hatch into full grown adult flies. Small flies often mistaken for baby houseflies are really adult *tachinid* flies which, unlike the housefly, are beneficial to man by being parasitic upon other insects.

The fly is of the order *Diptera,* from the Greek meaning "two wings."   J. M. C.

SEE ALSO: ARTHROPODA, INSECTA, LARVA, METAMORPHOSIS

Flycatcher These birds are perching birds. They may be medium or small in size with fairly large heads. Bristles are on either side of their bills. Most species have grayish-brown feathers on their backs. Breasts may be cream or yellow. Some have crests on their heads.

All these birds have a flat, broad bill with a slight downward hook at the tip. Flycatchers eat insects. Perching on branches, they dart out to capture any insects flying past. This type of feeding gives the flycatcher its name.

Three to five cream-colored eggs, spotted in some species, are laid in a nest. Nests of leaves, bark, feathers, and fur are built in a cavity, like a hollow in a tree.

Flycatchers belong to the family Tyranidae, which occurs only in America. There are around 400 species with about 30 of them living in the United States. The phoebes and the kingbirds are also flycatchers.   J. C. K.

fications of the two missing wings are called *halteres* and are rod-shaped organs used for balance in flight. Flies have compound eyes and sometimes three auxiliary eyes called *ocelli.* They eat by means of a *proboscis*—a long sucking tube that includes the mouth. The fly breathes through holes along its body called *spiracles.*

Flies can walk upside down on the ceiling because their feet have cushions, called *pulvilli,* which attach themselves to smooth surfaces by tiny sticky hairs.

Crane fly

Buchsbaum

An American flycatcher

Conversion Factors to Metric Measurement

Length

1 inch = 25.4 millimeters (mm) exactly
1 inch = 2.54 centimeters (cm) exactly
1 foot = 0.3048 meters (m) exactly
1 yard = 0.9144 meters (m) exactly
1 mile = 1.609344 kilometers (km) exactly

Area

1 square inch = 6.4516 square centimeters (cm^2) exactly
1 square foot = 0.092903 square meters (m^2)
1 square yard = 0.836127 square meters (m^2)
1 square acre = 0.404686 hectares (ha)
1 square mile = 2.58999 square kilometers (km^2)

Cubic Measure

1 cubic inch = 16.387064 cubic centimeters (cm^3) exactly
1 cubic foot = 0.0283168 cubic meters (m^3)
1 cubic yard = 0.764555 cubic meters (m^3)

US Liquid Measure

1 fluid ounce = 29.5735 milliliters (ml)
1 fluid ounce = 0.2957 deciliters (dl)
1 pint = 0.473176 liters (l)
1 gallon = 3.78541 liters (l)

US Dry Measure

1 pint = 0.550610 liters (l)
1 bushel = 35.2391 liters (l)

Weight

1 grain = 0.0647989 grams (g)
1 ounce = 28.3495 grams (g)
1 pound = 0.453592 kilograms (kg)
1 short ton = 0.907185 metric tons (t)
1 UK ton = 1.01605 metric tons (t)

Temperature

To convert Fahrenheit to Centigrade (Celsius) complete the following
equation. $(F° - 32) \times 5 \div 9 = C°$